G000253605

FISHING FOR BEGINNERS

FISHING FOR BEGINNERS

by

Maurice Wiggin

DIAGRAMS BY W. J. PÉZARE
AND 8 PLATES

J. M. DENT & SONS LTD

Printed in Great Britain
by
Latimer, Trend & Co. Ltd · Whitstable
for
J. M. DENT & SONS LTD
Aldine House · Bedford Street · London
First published by Phoenix House Ltd 1953
Revised edition 1958
Reprinted 1960
First published in this edition 1962
Reprinted 1964, 1967, 1971

ISBN: 0 460 02006 4

To
FARMER TOM JONES
of Bramshott Chase
in the County of Hampshire
KEENEST *and* KINDEST
(and ever a boy at heart)
this book is affectionately
dedicated

Contents

7

Illustrations

PART I: FISHING IS FUN

~~~~~~

1. A World Apart

~~~~~~

I HAVE BEEN fishing ever since I was a small and rather skinny boy, about six or seven years old. I hope to be fishing when I am a very old man. I never heard of anyone giving up fishing. It grows on you.

It is only fair to warn you right at the start that if fishing really does take hold of you, you will be in all sorts of trouble. You will find yourself thinking about fishing when you ought, by rights, to be thinking about quite different things—for instance, if you are a boy, such things as algebra or irregular verbs. Because there is not much doubt that fishing is many times more interesting than algebra, or even Greek. If I had paid more attention to algebra and less to angling, I might have been a richer man now. But not a happier.

Well, that is a risk you have to take when you take up fishing. True, there have been fine fishermen who were also very successful in other matters—Sir Edward Grey, for instance, who managed to be a good scholar and even Foreign Secretary, as well as a prince among anglers. But most of us have only enough *nous* (a Greek word which I cannot translate) to do about one thing very well, and if you have to choose between fishing and something else, it is a fearful dilemma. I solved my own dilemma years ago, in favour of fishing.

If you do the same you will never really regret it, though of course you will have pangs and anxious moments now and then. But all the other troubles will recede as time passes, and the delight of fishing will never recede. I can promise you that.

Because an angler's world is a world apart. It has its own problems, of course—every world does—and you spend your whole life trying to solve them. But it is not a rather silly world of meanness and humbug and vainglory, like some. It is a world of mystery, silence, and beauty, a world of unending adventure, and a world of solitude. Every angler's world is a private world.

This is the most important ingredient in the multitude of ingredients which make the angler's happiness. You are on your own. It is true that many people like to fish together, lining the banks of a river at ten-yard intervals, catching as many little fish as they can as fast as they can, in competition for some trumpery prize. But that isn't fishing as I know it. The real fisherman spurns the very idea of fishing competitions.

The real angler goes out on his own. He does not care very much for the life of towns. He is a solitary bird, your true fisher, and if he sees another angler approaching he is not very well pleased. This is unsociable, but there it is. You don't take up fishing because you feel sociable. You take up fishing because (among other things) you enjoy solitude.

If you *don't* enjoy solitude don't take up fishing. Or at least don't bother with this book. This book is written by a man who loves solitude, for those who already feel the mysterious pull of the silent places, the remote and enchanted places, where nature keeps its own counsel and none of the catchwords that govern life in towns has any meaning. Even to begin to enjoy fishing you must have a fondness for the remote, still places, far away from towns.

There is another condition. To enjoy fishing to the full you must be able to catch fish. Well, naturally. That is what this book is for—to tell you *how* to catch fish. But curiously enough, although you will not enjoy fishing unless you sometimes catch fish, it is also true that catching fish is not the *chief* pleasure of fishing. At least, I have not found it so. For me, from boyhood until now, the chief pleasure of fishing has lain in the escape it offers from the strident life of towns. The silence and mystery of water always makes me happy whether or not I catch fish. To catch a fish just puts the seal on what is in any case a happy day.

There are birds abounding—many more birds than you seem to see away from the waterside. I have seen otters, a badger or two, foxes, stoats, and weasels—and, of course, innumerable hares and voles. Voles are very nice indeed. They are *not* rats—everyone hates rats, of course, and rightly—but voles are delightful, velvety creatures that potter about quite unconcernedly, willing to live and let live. And, of course, you see three birds in particular which are wonderful enough to make any day a happy day: the kingfisher, the dipper, and the heron. The kingfisher, Halcyon, is surely the loveliest bird in our lovely land. He flashes across the water like a bar of blue electricity. Of course he is shy—all wild things are shy—but if you practise being silent and still, you can get on surprisingly familiar terms with Halcyon. I have even had him perch on the tip of my rod; the most wonderful catch I ever made.

Harry the heron is another favourite of mine. But I am not a favourite of his, nor will you be if you take up fishing. Harry is a fisher himself, and a first-rate one, and naturally he hates competition. But he is worth watching, all the same. If you can fish as well as Harry—or anything like a quarter as well—you will never go short of fish. After all, Harry depends on his catch, just as any deep-sea trawlerman. He has to fish to live. Watch how he stands there among the reeds, blending into his background in his tattered old shabby suit of greys and dusty browns. Silent he stands, one long spindly leg drawn up under him, peering down into the water until he sees a fish swimming innocently around his leg, no doubt thinking it a bit of tree or reed. Then *down* goes his great beak, *slash*! He never misses.

Yes, it is a great world you enter when you go fishing. A wonderful, beautiful, exciting world. You can keep your cricket pitches. Let me slip silently off, alone, or with one good, trusty friend at most, into the ever-fresh, ever-exciting world of the waterside.

What sort of fishing you will get depends a good deal on where you live. *Wherever* you live—even if you live in some big manufacturing city like Birmingham or Leeds—there is sure to be fishing to be had within easy reach. True, it may not be very *good* fishing, and perhaps you will have to search it out and make tedious journeys to reach it. But it is always worth the journey. I live in the country, and there is a lake full of fish within 200 yards of my cottage door. But when I was a boy, and for years and years after, to go fishing meant making a journey. For I was born and brought up in the industrial midlands; almost in the Black Country. I had to travel for my fishing, on foot or on my old bike. And it was never very good fishing when I got there— just the ordinary humdrum sort of fishing you get in the old canals and pit-pools of the midlands. Never mind: it was worth every turn of the pedals, every drop of rain that ran down my neck, every bead of sweat, and every blister.

I hope that you will be luckier than I. If you live in the west or north you may find trout-fishing on your doorstep, free. This is wonderful. And if you live in East Anglia, you will have on your doorstep what is perhaps the finest coarse fishing in the world. Good luck to you. Fishing is where you find it.

And this I know to be true. If you grow up with the modest, small-scale fishing of the less favoured parts of the country, and never know any better, you will be just exactly as happy as the chap who grows up on the lordly salmon rivers of the north and west. Every bit as happy. I, thank heaven, have known all sorts of fishing, and it would be idiotic to deny that a salmon is a finer fish than a roach. But if you never fish for anything but roach, you will never need regret it. Fair fishing—honest, decent, sportsmanlike fishing with rod and line that gives the fish a chance—fair fishing is equal fun wherever you find it. Even now, with all sorts of experience behind me, I am just as happy, just as excited, when I amble down to the lake to fish for little roach and rudd as when I carefully grease my expensive tapered line and take my fly rod to catch fighting trout. Fishing is fun, my friend, wherever you may be and *whoever* you may be. Far and away the finest fisher in my village is a rum old character who looks a real bag of bones and has been in more trouble in his time than a regiment of Russians. He doesn't own any fine tackle, he hasn't a penny to his name, and he isn't over-particular about shaving. But let him cut a hazel stick and lend him a hook ('lend.' Ha!) and he will show you just how to catch fish from places where you'd swear there *aren't* any fish. If only I could fish as well as he can, or alternatively if he could write more than his own name—what a book this would be!

Never mind, it's going to be as good a book as I can make it.

2. What You Need

YOU DON'T need much. But you can acquire as much as you like. It's entirely a matter of means, temperament, and opportunity.

When I first went fishing the only tackle I had was a common garden-cane for rod, a length of cotton for line, a matchstick for float, and a bent pin for hook. Even at that I was better off than some of my pals who could not bring themselves to spend a penny on a cane. They 'made do' with a hazel switch cut out of a hedge.

Well, you *can* catch fish with that sort of tackle—but only minnows and sticklebacks. There is nothing fatally wrong with the stick, the cotton, and the matchstick, but you really do need a proper *hook*. As I said, you *can* catch minnows and sticklebacks on bent-pin tackle, but that is because minnows and sticklebacks are very stupid and very greedy fish indeed. If you bait your bent pin with a small worm, a minnow will grab it and may hang on even when you pull him out of the water. But not all fish are so obliging, and the point is that you can't really *hook* a fish on a bent pin. It is neither sharp enough nor stiff enough. So one thing you simply must buy is a hook. And since the hook is the first thing to get lost or broken, you had better buy several while you are about it. It isn't really wise to go fishing without at least one spare hook.

There are all sorts and sizes of hooks, as there are all sorts and sizes of fish. Some fish have small mouths and it is not much good fishing for them with large hooks. On the other hand you can catch even a large-mouthed fish with a small hook. As a general rule you should use the smallest reasonable size of hook.

Now that may sound puzzling, but luckily there is a simple rule about hooks. If the *bait* is big, the hook must be rather big. If the bait is small the hook must be small.

Later in this book you will learn about baits (Chapter 5). When you have made up your mind about the most suitable bait, then you must choose a hook to suit. If, say, you are using a big worm to catch perch or bream which love big worms, or a big knob of bread-paste to catch chub or carp, then you will need a hook of about size 8. If you are using a small red worm, or a small pellet of paste such as roach and dace like, then you will need a smallish hook of size 12 or 14. If there are only small fish where you go fishing, such as small dace, rudd, roach, or bleak, then you will do best with a tiny morsel of bread-paste on a size 16 hook.

It's a funny thing, but the bigger the number the smaller the hook. Don't ask me why. People have been arguing about it for years, and many schemes have been put forward to simplify the numbering of hooks. But the old scale clings stubbornly to life, just as we hang on doggedly to our rum coinage while foreigners, who are cleverer though not nicer, have long since simplified life with the decimal system. Anyway, size 16 is the smallest you are ever likely to need. Smaller hooks than size 16 are made, but ignore them. Even if you get a bite with a hook smaller than size 16, it is long odds against your hooking the fish securely.

The biggest hook you are likely to need is about size 8. If I were you I should start off by buying two number 10, two number 12, and two number 14 hooks. Then you are fairly well set up. But if money is tight you can make do with a couple of size 12 hooks. I should say that size 12 is definitely the best all-round size, and if I were challenged to fish a whole season through with no other size than that, I shouldn't worry very much. But size 12 is rather on the big side for such small-mouthed, quick-biting fish as dace and little roach.

Most fishermen buy their hooks already tied—'whipped' is

the technical term—to lengths of gut or nylon. We can really stop talking about gut, although it is a traditional word in angling. For, nowadays, nylon has superseded gut for all practical purposes. You can still buy gut, of course, but nylon is vastly cheaper and at least as good. So let's just say nylon. It is very convenient to buy your hooks ready whipped to nylon, but you can save money by asking for *eyed* hooks—that is, hooks with a little metal eye or loop at the top of the shank—and tying them yourself to a bit of nylon. I almost always do.

Of course, if you decide to economize by buying eyed hooks, you will have to buy some nylon to tie them to. Ready-whipped hooks-to-gut are tied to nylon of varying thicknesses, from exceedingly fine to moderately stout. The thicker the stronger—but the finer the more nearly invisible. You have to balance the one desirable factor against the other. My own preference is always for the finest gauge that it is reasonable to use. I would rather hook a fish and lose it through the nylon breaking, than fail to interest a fish at all just because my nylon was so thick that it made the fish suspicious. Never forget that fish are terribly suspicious creatures. They have to be. So buy fairly thin nylon—not fantastically thin but fairly—and always remember that it will break easily, so you simply must handle it with constant care.

You had better ask for nylon of a medium thickness to begin with. What *I* call 'medium' is the grade known as 4X. Some anglers would laugh like horses to hear this described as medium. Some very expert anglers use nylon of 8X and even 10X—really almost invisibly thin—and very well indeed they manage it. But since you are only just beginning to fish, it is more than likely that you will be a bit 'ham-handed' with your first few fish, and you would certainly lose a fish hooked on such fine stuff. So ask for 4X or even 3X, which is noticeably thicker and a great deal stronger.

The best plan, for economy, is to buy a few eyed hooks and a length of nylon of 2 lb. breaking strain. Then you can tie your own hooks on and make your own casts. In Chapter 23 you will learn how to tie nylon. It is terribly tricky stuff to use if you *don't* take the trouble to learn and use the proper knots, I warn you. That is why some anglers have turned against it. But on the other hand, if you will take the trouble to use the proper knots you will never have the least trouble with nylon, and many of us find it better in every way than the old-fashioned gut, and many times cheaper.

When you have bought your little spool of nylon, cut off as many pieces each two feet long as you have hooks, and tie the hooks on carefully with the turle knot. (See Chapter 23.) Then you are set up for hooks.

Now you must have a line.

If a fish saw a big thick piece of gut or nylon leading to the bait on your hook he would come to the conclusion that there was something fishy about the whole business and leave your bait severely alone. You can't blame him. That is why you use fine nylon down there near the hook. But the line that leads from the hook-length to the rod doesn't need to be so fine because the fish doesn't see it, as a rule. So you can manage very well with a line of 5–6 lb. breaking strain—a line made of nylon, plaited silk, or even flax: it doesn't matter much, at this stage. You need about fifty yards. This is called your reel line, and it leads us naturally to your reel.

The reel is just a bit of simple machinery by means of which you can either let out more line or wind it in. You can buy a reel made of metal, wood, or plastic for a very few shillings, and it will be perfectly satisfactory. All you need ask of a reel is that it revolves freely. Don't forget that a reel is all the better for *a drop* of oil now and again, but only a drop.

Wind your line on to the reel carefully, keeping an even, light tension and making sure that it is spread evenly from side to side of the reel spool—not all bunched up in the middle or at one side. Otherwise it won't run easily.

If you can't afford a reel don't despair. I fished for years and years without one. In fact, I would go so far as to say that it is a very good thing to learn to fish without a reel as the great roach fishers of the Thames and Lea always did. If you can control a good fish without a reel on your rod you will have acquired 'hands,' that subtle quality which horsemen know all about. True, it is nice to have a reel. Not having one rather limits your fishing, and if you hook a really good fish you more or less *need* a reel—unless you have the hands of a master. But there are thousands upon thousands of anglers who have never owned a reel in their lives and yet have managed to get a great deal of fun out of fishing and to catch a great many respectable fish. Even today, hundreds of thousands of anglers on the Continent of Europe never use a reel. I have fished with Frenchmen and Dutchmen and Germans who managed without and managed exceedingly well.

But it *is* nice to own one, I admit. And it makes you master of a lot of interesting water that you simply could not fish without a reel. So buy one if you can rise to it. And don't worry if you can't, just yet.

Next you will need a float. At least, you will *want* a float. And quite rightly. It is perfectly possible to fish successfully for a whole lifetime without a float, as it is possible to fish without a reel. But half the fun of fishing comes from watching the float—well, perhaps not *half*, but a good proportion. In the whole funfair of delights that constitutes fishing there is no one solitary thing that gives so much unalloyed pleasure to so many people as watching a float. It is perhaps the very essence of the fun of fishing. So a float we must certainly have.

The float does two jobs. It tells you, of course, when a fish is biting. But it also has another job—it enables you to hang your bait at the right depth in the water. This is very important indeed, as you will soon realize.

There are literally hundreds of different sorts of float, all utterly delightful to look at. Frankly, I have bought so many floats in my time that I have to keep a lot of them hidden away in a box, or otherwise I spend so much time just looking at them, admiring their elegant shapes and pretty colours, that I should get no work done. You can buy a float at any tackle shop, or you can make your own as easily as falling into the river. If you are buying your first, choose a medium-sized one—not a whopper, glorious though they look with their fat cork bodies and gleaming red-and-green paint, nor a really tiny quill that looks like a toothpick. But one in between. It is *always* better to have a float that is a bit on the small side. So if you are buying your first tell the man in the tackle shop that you want a float which will carry two split shot. He will know exactly what that means, even if you don't—yet.

Now for the ROD. This is the most interesting part of your tackle. I must watch my step and be very careful not to set off on a long harangue about rods, or we shall never get down to the water. For rods fascinate me. I have been collecting them all my life, and I shall always be collecting them, swopping them, making them, giving them away, handling them, altering them, and just simply looking at them. They are glorious things, the most delightful tools man ever made, the instruments of joy, the passport to pleasure, the wand that sets you free. There I am, you see, off already. I must check this and get down to the hard facts about the sort of rod *you* want, to begin with.

You *can* spend a great deal of money on rods. I've done so myself. But the simple truth is that for most of the ordinary sort of freshwater fishing which you are likely to do in your first year or two, almost any old rod will serve. Don't, for goodness' sake, let me stop you if you intend to buy one of the lovely, glossy rods in the tackle shop. But don't, on the other hand, feel the least bit depressed if you can't afford one yet. At a pinch you can catch fish with any old branch cut out of a hedge. I've seen it done time and again, and I've done it myself.

On the other hand, there is no getting away from the fact that you will have much more fun if you own a nice rod of which you can be proud. But what makes a nice rod? Not the shiny varnish which rod-makers slap on, assuredly not that. Rods should *not* shine; the flash of an over-painted rod has 'put down' many a fish. No, the most important thing in your rod is *balance*. There are three factors to consider in buying a rod: *length, action,* and *balance.* Of these three, balance is by far the most important at this stage in our fishing career. Balance is what matters most in all fishing tackle. Every item of your equipment—rod, reel, line, float, sinker, and hook—must be in harmony. Must balance. A rod that is too heavy for you will soon take the fun out of your fishing—sooner, I think, than any other single factor, including rain, which no true angler really minds. A rod that is *top-heavy* is almost as bad, because although it may not weigh very much all-in, if there is too great a proportion of that weight in the top half of the rod it will soon begin to tire you. A rod that is *bottom-heavy* is not so bad, but it is still to be avoided. It is a certainty that you will not hook half so many possible bites if the rod does not feel absolutely comfortable in your hand. It is worth going to a lot of trouble to make sure that it *is* so.

In the perfectly balanced outfit, the 'point of balance' is just where your hand grips the butt of the rod. When you are trying a rod in a tackle shop, ask the salesman to fit a suitable reel to it. Do this, even if you have no intention of buying a reel. (If the salesman refuses, walk out and find another shop.) Try balancing the rod on one finger, like a seesaw. It should balance perfectly when your finger is just in front of the reel (just *above* the reel, that is). If it does this, you can be sure that the rod will sit comfortably in your hand through a long day's fishing.

Now if you are going to buy your first rod, there is something you must settle before you get anywhere near the shop. You *must* know what kind of rod you want. Otherwise you will be lost the moment you see all the lovely rods set out in their racks —lost and helpless, as I have been many and many a time: and you will come out with the wrong rod, that's a certainty.

In a good tackle shop you will find rods for general 'bottom-fishing,' as ordinary float fishing is called, rods for spinning, rods for fly-fishing, rods for pike-fishing, and rods for sea-fishing. All you are interested in just now is a rod for general bottom-fishing. So don't waste time trying rods which would be almost useless to you. Tell the man behind the counter that you want a light rod for general bottom-fishing, and he will know exactly what to show you. The rod you want is very often called a 'roach rod'—but in fact you can catch a lot of other fish with it in addition to roach.

Now general bottom-fishing rods vary a great deal. You can buy them in all lengths from about ten up to fourteen feet or even more. Ten feet is a good length for a boy: twelve feet ideal for a man. The rod will be made in either two or three pieces— probably three, which is more convenient for carrying around. The butt joint and the middle joint will, or should, be made of 'whole cane'—that is to say, simple hollow bamboo, just like a garden cane. But the top joint will not, for hollow bamboo, although very satisfactory for the thicker parts, has not the stamina for the top joint, which bears most of the weight of the fish and flexes a great deal. The top joint will be made either of a solid, tough wood like lancewood, hickory, or that wonderful, rare wood called greenheart, or of built cane. A tip of built cane will put the price of the rod up a great deal, but it is worth it, for with a built cane tip you get a much quicker action on the strike. But greenheart or lancewood is perfectly satisfactory, and such a rod should only cost some £2.

If such a price is beyond you, rummage around in all the

second-hand shops you can find until you unearth an old green-heart trout rod, anything from eight to eleven feet long. You can often pick up such old rods for a matter of a few shillings, and they will serve you wonderfully well for float fishing, although rather on the whippy side.

Well, now you have your rod, line, float, and hooks—and perhaps a reel, or perhaps not. There is only one other item which you simply *must* have, and that is a tin of split shot to act as a sinker.

You can add to that list of tackle, and you probably will. You can go on collecting items all your life—such things as a landing net, a keep-net, disgorgers, spare reels, and lines and rods—oh, all manner of things. But I would never pretend that they were strictly necessary. Just as you can play a jolly good game of football with no equipment whatsoever beyond some sort of ball, so you can fish successfully with no bought equipment beyond a hook. If I had one hook in my pocket, and no other tackle whatsoever, I would still go fishing. I would cut a long sapling for rod, tie on to it a few yards of thin string or stout thread, make a float out of a matchstick and a bit of cork— and, with luck, I should catch fish.

You will get what tackle you can afford. So long as it contains one real hook, you can catch fish. And now, let's go fishing.

3. A-hunting We Will Go

EVERY SPORT has its rules. Luckily, the rules of fishing are few in number and easy to learn, though not always easy to remember in the excitement of the chase. In fact, they are no more than simple common sense. But if you break these few simple rules, you will never make a fisherman.

The first and by far the most important rule of fishing is this: *Don't frighten the fish.* Fish are very easily frightened, and a frightened fish will never bite. Never.

Remember always that fishing is a sort of hunting. You are trying to persuade a wild thing to eat a bait in which you have hidden a hook. Now in the course of nature wild things are suspicious of everything and everybody. They have to be. The first thing a fish learns is that it is surrounded by enemies. Never forget that nature, so gentle and beautiful and peaceful to the eye of the tourist or rambler, is really a bloodthirsty jungle in which every living thing is preying on some other living thing. Only in the human world do reason and deliberate kindness operate. Wild things are wild: no kidding, no kid gloves, no holds barred, no pity, no mercy.

Naturally, then, a wild thing is always on the jump for possible enemies. That is why you have to fool a fish. You have to trick him into thinking that your bait is a morsel of food which he can gobble up without risk to himself. For although fish are very often hungry, caution will defeat hunger almost every time.

Some fish are more cunning than others, but all fish are alike in one respect—they don't like the look of human beings. No one yet knows for certain just how well a fish's eyes work. Some say they are short-sighted. Some say they are colour-blind

—some say they are not. But it is safe to state that if you can see a fish, that fish can see you (if he happens to be looking your way, of course). So you *must* keep out of sight.

I don't mean that the fish will recognize you. He won't mutter to his companions: 'Ah, there goes a fourth-form boy wearing a Second Eleven blazer and grey socks. He's up to no good.' No, he won't know if you are a fourth-form boy or an old man of forty odd, like me. But he *will* know, at a glance, that you are something strange and big and dangerous, and he will be off like a flash.

This means that you must not stand right at the edge of the water, though the temptation to do so is almost irresistible. Always keep as far back from the edge as you can. Of course, you have to get *fairly* near to the water or you wouldn't see your float. But approach the water carefully, stealthily, above all *quietly*, remembering that you are a hunter stalking his prey. For that is just what you are, and if you forget to behave with a hunter's cunning, you might just as well stay at home for all the fish you will catch. Well, perhaps that is a shade drastic: you can generally manage to catch *something*, some trifling little tiddler of a fish; for very small, very young fish haven't yet learned the lesson of fish life. But we're setting out to be real, serious anglers, I hope; and real, serious big fish aren't to be caught as tiddlers are. They know better.

Keep as *low* as you can, even if it means looking slightly ridiculous by stooping and crouching as you move. Never mind if a spectator sniggers. You're not out to please spectators, but to catch fish. And do your fishing sitting down wherever it is possible. If you must stand up, try to make sure that there is some sort of *cover*, either between you and the water, or behind you. 'Cover behind you' sounds odd, I know, but it is a fact that if you are standing with your back to a bush, a tree, or a clump of tall grasses, or a high bank, the fish won't notice you. After all, the fish is used to the bush or the tree or the tall grass or the high bank: I expect he sees it as a vague blur on the skyline. Anyway, he is used to it. It is when someone or something suddenly appears on the skyline that he gets worried. It is *movement* that frightens fish.

So never forget that the very first thing in fishing is to approach the water as quietly and craftily as you possibly can. This is just the point where almost everyone goes wrong. Almost every time I go fishing I see someone dashing along to the waterside, so keen to get started that he can't wait a moment. Whenever you see a chap fitting up his rod as he goes along, you can almost take it for granted that he is going to have a blank day, poor fellow. Mind you, I've done it myself, time and again, before I knew better. I very well understand that terrible eagerness to get started, to get the line on the water. But believe me, this is exactly where people go fatally wrong. If you really want to catch fish, you simply *must* control that desperate eagerness and cut out the mad dash to the waterside.

Keep on telling yourself that *this is hunting*. Think like a hunter. Practise moving quietly and unobtrusively. If you can come up on someone without his knowing that you are approaching, then you stand a fair chance of surprising a fish. I must say that I still take a pleasure in being able to get right up to a man without his knowing that I am anywhere near him. It is the first rule of life for all hunters, and the keen angler practises it all the time, even when he is not fishing. People who bounce about never make good anglers.

You see, a fish has not only keen sight, but an extremely keen sense of vibrations. I don't mean hearing as we understand hearing; but it amounts to hearing, or even more so. Along the sides of every fish runs a line—not necessarily visible—which is called the lateral line, or median line. In some fishes you can see it. Scientists believe that this line consists of nerve-endings which are extremely sensitive to changes of pressure in the water—that is, to vibrations. A sort of radar, in fact; though it might be more accurate to call them a sort of hydrophone.

Now if you stamp on the bank, the vibrations which you set up travel through the water at high speed, and are picked up by the 'radar' of every fish for yards around. So move quietly. Keep low. Use every scrap of cover. And, finally, don't be in too much of a hurry to begin.

These are the first rules of fishing. Quite simple, aren't they? —and great fun, too. When you have consciously practised moving silently and unobtrusively for some time it becomes second nature, and you will be surprised how much more fun you can get out of such a simple pastime as a country walk. Your eyes will be getting more observant, your ears sharper, and you will begin to see sights which you wouldn't see in a lifetime if you were the sort of chap who stamps around advertising his presence by thumping boots and shrill whistle. You will see rare birds and beasts at close quarters—I once saw a wonderful fight between two weasels, and I've seen the rare badger several times—and gradually you will begin to enjoy the natural scene to the full.

There are just two more basic rules to learn. One is: *use the sun*. Never forget that a shadow cast on the water frightens fish just the same as a man waving his arms on the bank. Always try to fish with the sun in your face. It isn't always possible, of course; but if you *must* fish with the sun at your back, try to make yourself as small as possible—and keep your rod low.

Lastly, *keep as still as you can*. Even when you have wormed your way into a good fishing position, don't be in a hurry to start waving your rod about. Sit still for a few minutes—and then the fish, even if they see you, will take you for granted as a part of the landscape. It is sudden movement, every time, that frightens fish. I often spend ten minutes in covering the last ten yards to my chosen fishing position—and when I have reached it I stay still and watch the water. Let the heron be your guide. He *always* catches fish.

PART II: FLOAT FISHING

~~~~~~

4. Business before Pleasure

~~~~~~

MOST FISHING is float fishing. There are other ways of catching fish, and delightful they are. There is spinning and there is fly-fishing, both of which we shall come to in good time. And even if you are just fishing with ordinary baits it is perfectly possible to catch fish without a float on your line. But a float makes it easier and far more interesting. At any rate, in this chapter we are going to talk about the float.

A float, as we have seen, serves two purposes. Firstly and most obviously, it serves as an indicator which tells you when a fish is taking your bait. Secondly, it enables you to suspend the bait at the right depth in the water.

What is 'the right depth'? The right depth is the depth at which the fish are feeding. What that depth is depends partly on the kind of fish you are angling for and partly on other factors— I explain these other factors in the chapters devoted to separate species of fish. But you will realize that if you do *not* use a float your bait will go straight to the bottom of the water, and stay there. This is all very well for some species of fish, which feed right on the bottom. But other fish feed at varying depths, all the way from the bottom to the surface of the water, and you want to be able to present your bait to the fish at the level on which he is feeding. By moving the float up or down the line, you can decide for yourself just how near to the bottom your bait shall hang.

Another thing. If you just throw in your baited hook without a float on the line, it will tend to get stuck on the bottom. If the bottom is soft and muddy, or carpeted with decaying leaves, it may sink out of sight—and then no fish will find it, with the just-possible exception of a scavenging eel. If you are fishing a river, you may want your bait to travel downstream with the current, in the way that much natural food travels down to waiting fish. This it cannot do, plainly, if it is stuck on the bottom. For all the above reasons, you will find a float useful as well as interesting.

Now let us start by fixing up your tackle. Always do this well back from the waterside—ten yards at least, fifty yards for preference. First tie the hook, which is already attached to its 'hook-length' of nylon, to the cast. The cast is another length of nylon, anything from one yard to two yards long, and of slightly stouter gauge than the hook-length. It is slightly stouter than the hook-length for the simple reason that if you get caught up in a snag on the bottom, or a tree, or even a big fish, and have to break your tackle, it will break at the weakest point. If the weakest point is the hook-length, then you will only lose your hook—and that is a good deal cheaper than losing your cast and float as well. As I go around I find many a float and cast decorating trees and bushes, usually just out of reach. These were the property of anglers who did not bother to make sure that the hook-length was the weakest part of their tackle. Fortunately, I don't mind climbing trees, and I come by quite a fair bit of tackle that way.

Right. You have a cast, looped at each end, about a yard long for preference. (Remember that far the cheapest way of getting casts is to cut them from a spool of nylon and loop them yourself. But you must use the knots described in Chapter 23, or you will be asking for trouble.)

Figure 1 shows you how to fix the hook-length to the cast, the cast to the line, and the float to the cast. Now you must pinch some split shot to the cast.

FIG. I

Split shot, as you may guess, consists of shot-gun pellets which have been *almost* split in half. You fix one to your cast by laying the cast in the V-shaped split or groove and closing the shot over the nylon fairly tightly. You are supposed to use a small pair of pliers to do this, and indeed it is a useful tool to have around for several reasons, including taking out a hook which has lodged deeply either in a fish or elsewhere. But I will confess that I have been using my front teeth for this operation for more than thirty years, and funnily enough my front teeth are the only good teeth I have left. However, please yourself. Use a hammer if you like. If you *do* use your teeth, try not to bite right through the cast. It's maddening.

The split shot, like the float, does two jobs for the price of one. It ensures that your baited hook swims as low in the water as you want it to—as you can imagine, a strong current would tend to lift the hook, and you often need weight to keep it down. Its other job is to make the float 'cock.'

If you drop a float on to the water it lies flat. All of it floats. Now this is no good to you at all when you are fishing. If a fish pulls at your bait, he will immediately feel quite a lot of resistance from that flat-lying float. He will certainly come to the very sensible conclusion that there is something odd about the bait, and he will drop it. You want your float to tell *you* that there is a

31

fish touching your bait, not to tell the fish that there is an angler attached to it. So the float must be able to slide downwards through the water with the least possible resistance. It will do this if it is riding in the water more or less vertical—that is just why floats are streamlined. And that is why you must nip on to your cast just enough split shot to make your float ride upright in the water: or, to use the technical term, to 'cock.'

How many split shot you will need depends partly on the size and the buoyancy of your float, and partly on the strength of the current. I have already mentioned that you ought to aim at the smallest float that will do the job—because the bigger the float, the more lead you will need to cock it; and the heavier the 'business end' of your tackle becomes, the more likely is the fish to become suspicious.

Of course, if you are fishing a fast-flowing, deep river, you must use a lot of lead to keep your bait down in the current, and hence you must use a biggish float (because a lot of lead would pull a smaller float right under the water). On a gently flowing stream you can manage with much less lead—and therefore you can use a smaller float. When fishing still water, such as ponds, lakes, and canals, you can use a really small float, the smaller the better, which can be cocked by one or at most two small split shot.

Only by trial and error can you find out just how many split shots are needed to cock your float. Nip the first shot on to your nylon about eighteen inches above the hook; some go lower than that, but I like to have a fair length of unweighted nylon so that a fish will play around with the bait without getting suspicious. But I must tell you in all honesty that many fine anglers put the first shot nearer to the hook than that—a foot away, or even less. I personally think eighteen inches is about right. Nip the other shots—as many as are needed to make the float cock—at intervals above the first. Some bunch them all together within a few inches. I prefer to space them out a good deal, with an interval between each of about six inches. But they can be much nearer together than that, and if you are fishing shallow water they will have to be.

You want just about three-quarters of an inch of the tip of your float to be showing above water. But don't wait until you reach the waterside where you intend to fish to find out how many shot are needed to do this. Experiment at home. The water-butt is a perfect place to experiment. I have tried it in the bath—but not since I hooked myself.

(By the way, if ever you want to take split shot *off* the cast, you will find it quite a tricky little operation. The theory is that you open up the shot with your thumbnail or a knife. I can only say, sadly, that my thumbnail is too soft, and when I use a knife it often goes just that fraction too far and frays the cast. The ideal, of course, is not to nip a shot on until you are quite sure that the float will carry it.)

Now let's just run through the drill of assembling your tackle. Then we can start catching fish, or trying to.

Put up your rod by fitting the joints together. Very simple. Too easy, you say. But actually it isn't as easy as all that. You can lessen your chances of catching fish by putting your rod up in the wrong way. Worse still, you can ruin your rod.

Each joint of your rod ends in a brass ferrule: one ferrule fits into another. Now obviously, when you assemble your rod you must see that the rings through which the reel-line runs are exactly in line, from butt to tip. If they are not the line will not run easily through the rings, you will find it needlessly difficult to make a clean cast, and almost impossible to make your float travel smoothly downstream; and you will find your line wearing out far too soon, owing to friction against the rod rings. When you have assembled your rod, hold it up to your eye like a telescope, and squint along the rings to make certain that they are precisely in line.

When you come to take your rod apart at the end of the day's fishing, make quite sure that you grip each joint as near to the ferrule as you can possibly get your hands. Otherwise you may loosen the fit of the wood within the ferrule; you will certainly strain the rod and possibly start it warping. If the ferrules are too tight a fit and you find you cannot pull the joints apart with a reasonable pressure, then the trick is to light a match and gently warm the outer ferrule, turning it for a few seconds in the flame so that the heat is evenly distributed. This will cause the outer ferrule to expand, and then it is easier to pull the joints apart. If you find your ferrules tend to stick like that, rub the inner ferrule in your hair or on the side of your nose before you put up your rod. This gives it a slight film of grease, which is all the lubricant it should need.

Anyway, we now have your rod assembled, though I admit we made rather a long-winded job of it. Now fit the reel and thread the line up through the rings, *missing none*, and draw a couple of yards through the top ring. If you have to lay the rod on the ground in order to do this, make sure that the reel is not lying in a patch of dust or grit, and that the reel handles are uppermost. Tie your cast to your reel line, using the knot shown in Chapter 23, and we are almost done.

But not quite. Your next step must be to find out the depth of the water. This is essential because most fish feed on or near the bottom: you have, therefore, to set your float so that the bait hangs just clear of the bottom.

There are two ways of plumbing the depth. One is by trial and error. If the float lies flat on the water it is too far away from the hook. The split shot are lying on the bottom and therefore they cannot pull the float into a cocked position. The remedy is to pull the cast out of the water and slide the float down nearer to the hook. Keep on experimenting, moving the float only an inch or so at a time, until it just rides nicely upright. You can then be sure that it will present your bait to the fish where most

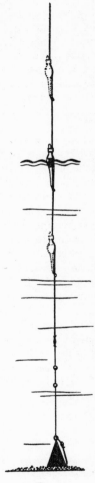

FIG. 2

of them expect to find their food—just clear of the bottom. (Of course, you don't actually have any bait on your hook while conducting this necessary experiment.)

The second way is to use a plummet. This is merely a lump of lead with a bit of cork let into it. You can easily make one. You slip your hook through a hole in the plummet and embed the point in the bit of cork; swing it out over the water; and lower it *gently* at the spot where you intend to fish. You will feel when it touches the bottom. Now keep the line taut and as nearly vertical as you can manage. If your float is above the surface of the water, withdraw the tackle and move it down towards the hook until it is just—but only just—submerged when the plummet rests on the bottom and the line is kept taut. Thus, you know that when you remove the plummet the float will ride properly and your bait will hang about half an inch from the bottom, which is just about right to start with. (If the float disappears when the plummet touches bottom, you must, of course, slide it back up the cast away from the hook.)

Important! This operation of plumbing the depth, though essential, must be carried out as quietly as possible. Lower the hook into the water, and withdraw it as slowly and gently as you can, disturbing the water as little as possible. If you start by making a splash, you can say good-bye to any decent fish.

Now you are absolutely ready to start fishing in earnest, or rather you would be if you had any bait on your hook. What about bait, then? Let's consider.

Fig. 2a

5. Baits and Ground-baiting

But every fish loves not each bait alike,
Although sometimes they feed upon the same;
But some do one, and some another seek,
As best unto their appetite do frame,
The Roach, the Bream, the Carp, the Chub and Bleak,
With paste or corn, their greedy hunger tame,
The Dace, the Ruffe, the Gudgeon and the rest
The smaller sort of crawling worms love best.

The Chavender or Chub do more delight
To feed on tender cheese or cherries red,
Black snails, their bellies slit to show the white,
Or grasshoppers that skip in every mead.
The Perch, the Tench, and Eel, do rather bite
At great red worms, in field or garden bred,
That have been scoured in moss or fennell rough
To rid their filth, and make them hard and tough.

JOHN DENNYS, *Secrets of Angling*, 1613.

'A WORM AT one end and a fool at the other.' That is how the great Doctor Johnson described anglers, in his nasty, bad-tempered way. And I suppose most non-anglers think of worms when they think of anglers. Fortunately, there need be no connection between the two. I personally hate using worms as a bait, and I honestly cannot remember when I last did so. And it will be a long long time before I use them again. So much for the 'traditional' bait, the bait which everyone who knows nothing about fishing *thinks* we use.

Some of us do, of course; many of us. Worms are a first-rate bait for almost any fish that swims. If you have no objection to impaling a worm on a hook and keeping it wriggling in the water until it dies or is taken by a fish, go ahead, and good luck to you. I just do not happen to like doing it, that is all. I dare say I'm a fool to feel like that about worms, which are pretty nearly the lowest form of life: maybe I am: I shouldn't be surprised. But the fact is that I loathe live-baiting of any and every kind. Live-baiting always involves keeping some living thing in misery for a fairly long time—whether it be a small roach or gudgeon or minnow which you are using to catch predatory fish like pike or perch, or just a miserable little worm. I have done it, time and again: but one lives and learns, and a man is entitled to change his mind. I've changed mine. Never again will I use live-bait. And that includes worms.

It even includes maggots, though in this case even I cannot honestly pretend that I have any tender feeling for the maggot. Not that I really have any tender feeling for the worm, mark you, but it is just conceivable that a worm might have feelings, and I don't see why I should be horribly cruel even to a worm, so I stay on the safe side and leave them alone. Maggots, of course, are perfectly vile. My objection to using maggots has nothing to do with their feelings, if any. I just hate them. Horrid, wriggling, smelly, beastly things. I used to use them—in fact, I used to breed my own, which is perfectly easy. Once the lid came off the maggot tin and the things got loose in the picnic basket: I'll never forget that. No, they are filthy little creepers, and I don't use them any more.

But let us understand one another. I'm going to tell you how to use worms and maggots as bait, because there is absolutely no reason why you should share my prejudices, and I am the first to admit that as baits, worms and maggots take a lot of beating. So they will get their place in this brief chapter on baits.

But heaven be praised, there are plenty of fine baits apart from

worms and maggots. Chief and foremost among them is—
bread. There are fish which do not normally accept bread as a
bait, but there are vastly more fish which *do*, and gladly. All the
year round, from the opening of the coarse-fishing season on
16 June to the last day on 14 March, bread in one shape or
another appeals to lots of fine fish.

Fish are roughly divided into two classes—predatory fish
which will eat other living things (including fish), and non-
predatory fish which you might call vegetarians. Predators—
that is to say, fish which prey upon other fish—will not normally
look at bread baits, but they occasionally do. They are the
perch and the pike. But perch and pike *have* been caught on
bread. Chub too are really predatory fish: they eat minnows,
certainly, and insects, and will go at a live bait when they feel
like it. But the very best of baits for chub is based upon bread.
All the other fish—the 'vegetarians'—will take bread baits
eagerly. These are the roach, bream, dace, gudgeon, carp,
barbel, tench, ruffe, bleak, rudd, and one or two other fairly
uncommon sorts of fish which we need not bother about now.

I suppose it is not really wise to class them as 'vegetarians,'
even in jest, for all of them without exception will take a flesh
bait such as a worm or maggot, or a scrap of meat—and they
will all eat flies. But I call them 'the vegetarians,' privately, to
distinguish them from such clashing terrors as the perch and
pike, who are true cannibals, really, and would rather eat other
fish than anything.

Now here are the handy baits and the fish which will eat them,
at one time or another.

BREAD, either in the form of bread-paste, cubes of crust,
scraps of crust, or simple flakes of crumb, will be taken by
roach, chub, dace, bream, carp, rudd, bleak, gudgeon, ruffe,
barbel.

WORMS will catch all the fish mentioned above and also
perch, grayling, trout, salmon, and tench.

MAGGOTS (they are called gentles in the south of England, but they're maggots just the same) will catch every fish mentioned above, with the exception of salmon.

CHEESE is the champion bait for chub, and will quite often be taken by roach.

ELDERBERRIES in season are a magnificent bait for roach and dace, especially if elder-trees grow near the water, overhanging: or even if they don't. Chub will also take them, but if you are fishing for chub you should use a bigger bait.

HEMPSEED is a first-rate bait for roach and dace. You have to simmer it in a drop of water—and in a very old pot!—until it begins to split and the white kernel just shows. You can catch fish on a split shot nipped direct on to your hook, with the shank painted white, if you interest the fish by throwing in a few grains of hempseed first. Even a scrap of leather boot-lace will do the trick, and, like many another angler, I have had fish grab at the split shot on my line. This is a good bait—hempseed, I mean—at times, but you need to be mighty smart on the strike. Perhaps the very best combination is hempseed thrown into the swim and elderberry actually used on the hook. This gives you a bit more time to strike.

The baits named above will see you through the year happily. There are plenty of others, but those are the real standbys. The other—or, rather, just a few of them—are: Wasp grubs, caddis grubs, pearl barley, wheat (boiled), very small potatoes partly boiled to soften them (a good bait for carp), cherries (a great bait for chub, I hear, though I have never used them), weed itself—the fine water-weed that clings to such things as lock gates—bits of bacon or bacon rind, bits of fruit (bananas especially), peas cooked or raw, beans, and all manner of flies.

But bread is the great bait for me, and if you don't mind not catching perch and pike you can have a wonderful lifetime of fishing without ever using anything else. (In fact, I catch many perch and pike, but by spinning, not float fishing. There is a chapter on spinning in this book [Chapter 17].)

Bread-paste is perhaps the commonest way of using bread, and one of the very best. You simply take the crust off some stale bread, put it in a bit of *clean* rag (no, not your handkerchief), dip it in water until it is thoroughly soaked, squeeze all the water out, and knead it in your hand until it is of a nice consistency. Some anglers swear by very soft pastes, holding that the hook will more easily penetrate the fish's mouth if it doesn't have to fight its way first through a layer of stiff paste. Very true; but against that is the objection that soft paste washes off the hook in no time at all. In fast water soft paste is quite useless. I like it medium firm. Like many others, I mix in some flour when I am kneading my paste. It helps to give it a good firm consistency and possibly lightens it a little in colour. Custard powder is often added. I always add it myself—but I would not like to swear that it really and truly makes any difference. The coal miner who first showed me how to mix bread-paste when I was a lad used custard powder, and I suppose I got the idea that it was quite essential. It isn't.

However, when I'm fishing for *carp* (see Chapter 14) I like to add something sweet to my paste. Honey is the prime favourite for carp baits, and I really do think that the carp has a sweet tooth. Brown bread-paste mixed with honey—that is a wonderful carp lure; so is the little potato boiled until it is just beginning to get soft and you can embed the hook in it neatly without squashing it too much.

I know a great fisherman who never under any circumstances uses anything but bread-crust, cut up into little cubes, winter and summer—and autumn too. True, he fishes seriously only for roach—but he catches them, almost unfailingly. I like crust, too, but at a pinch I prefer a medium-stiff bread-paste, flavoured with a pinch of custard powder or nothing at all.

Well, those are the hook baits. When you have read the

chapters on various fish you will have made up your mind which baits you prefer to use. But by all means experiment on your own. There may be baits never yet tried which will prove wonderfully attractive to fish, and if you are the one who discovers them, your fame will be assured. For all I know, Old Joe toffee, or liquorice allsorts, may prove the finest bait ever known. It has never been tried . . .

But there is another sort of bait, known as the ground-bait, about which you should know something. This is not the bait you put on your hook. It is the bait which you throw into the water to encourage the fish to your swim—or to encourage them to remain if they are there already. In lakes and ponds you are not in any great need of ground-bait, though it can be a help; but in rivers you will find ground-bait a great help if not actually essential.

Now obviously, if you are going to toss food into the river, you have to be careful of two things. Firstly, you have to make sure that you give away only enough food to stimulate the fishes' appetite, not to gorge them. Secondly, you have to be sure that your hook bait is lying, or travelling, where your ground-bait has settled. This is not so easy.

The first point is taken care of if you make your ground-bait *look* more attractive than it really is. *Cloud* bait is the ideal—something which breaks up and dissolves in the water, forming a slowly sinking cloud of fine particles which smell right and taste right but are really not at all substantial. In still water this is the simplest thing: in fast water, such lightweight cloud stuff would be instantly washed away downstream, attracting fish *away* from you, if at all. You always need to consider just what sort of water yours is.

Let us assume that you are fishing still or very slow-moving water. Then you will use cloud ground-bait. You can buy it, or you can very easily make it—provided you get a bit of co-operation in the kitchen! The very best 'cloud' consists merely of bread dust. You cut all the crust off a stale old loaf—the staler the better—and cut the crumb into chunks or slices. Dry these out in an oven—but not a very hot oven: the bread must not be toasted. Then rub the hard slices together, or pound them, into dust. That's all. Keep it in a tin with a lid that really fits. All you have to do is to moisten it at the waterside and toss in fragments around your hook. It will sink slowly, breaking up as it goes down, and attracting fish in a wonderful way. When it reaches the bottom it lies around, forming a sort of pale whitish sheet, which fish spot very readily. They come along, nose around in it, and—we hope—soon find your baited hook.

Plain dried bread makes far the best 'cloud,' in my opinion. But if you run into any trouble about the bread (!) you can eke out with various substitutes. Try to include *some* bread—indeed, you must have a certain proportion—but bran is also very good, and you can actually use sand or sawdust to make up bulk. Crushed egg-shells are another useful ingredient—they show up very well and attract the ever-inquisitive fish. If your people keep poultry, shell meal will be very helpful for your cloud. But remember to include *some* bread—after all, you are trying to tickle the fishes' appetites, and they will not hang around indefinitely if there is *nothing* tasty in the ground-bait.

If you are fishing fast-flowing water, such 'cloud' is no good at all. You must have a stiffer mixture which will stick on the bottom, *gradually* dissolving. For this purpose there is nothing to beat the old mixture of bread-and-bran. You soak the bread in cold water, drain the water off and pulverize the bread, and mix in a lot of bran until you have a really tacky mixture. Throw in small balls of this at the head of your chosen swim—that is to say, the upstream end—so that it will drift down and come to rest just about where your hook is fishing. Remember, it *must* come to rest there, or you are simply wasting your time. A better way than throwing in lumps, if you are not certain of your ability to gauge the strength of the current, is to squeeze a lump around your split shot every time you make a cast. This will ensure that it breaks up more or less where you want it to.

One final rule about ground-baiting. *Little and often* is far better than throwing in huge dollops at the beginning and then no more for a long time. And always remember—your aim is to excite the fishes' appetite, not to satisfy it.

Some fish, such as carp and bream, respond much better if you methodically 'bait up' a pitch for them days in advance. But you may not have the opportunity of doing that, more's the pity.

I think we can now actually start fishing. About time!

6. Casting

You HAVE DONE everything but fish. Your tackle is correct for the fish you are after. You have plumbed the depth and thrown in, perhaps, your bit of ground-bait. All you have to do now is to cast in your baited hook and start fishing.

Easier said than done. Any fool, of course, *can* cast in—but the longer I fish the more I am surprised at the fearful mess people make of that simple act of casting. Eight casts out of ten end in a clumsy, splashing fall that must terrify every fish within yards.

Your aim is to drop your hook into the water where it will do most good and with the minimum of fuss and splash. *Force* is never necessary: technique is everything. Unfortunately, it is the most difficult thing to explain in printed words just how to make a good cast, though I could show you in five minutes at the waterside. (So could any good angler. Ask one if you have the chance. He will be delighted to show you.)

Of course, if you are fishing still water quite near to the bank it is simplicity itself. You just raise your rod, extending your arm to the side of your body, and with a *gentle* swing bring the hook over the right spot on the water and lower it gently in. Nothing to it.

But if you want to make a fairly long cast to the deeper water of the pool or lake—or if you are fishing a river and have to get your bait well out into the stream, then it is a bit more tricky. (You cannot do it at all, of course, without a reel.)

Figure 3 shows you how to start a long cast. Gather the line as shown in loops in the left hand (held very tightly) and swing

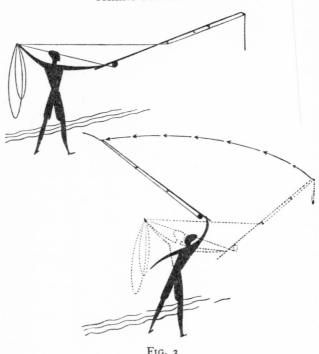

FIG. 3

the rod out over the water, gently but firmly. As you feel the baited hook beginning to fly out over the water, release the loops held in the left hand, one by one. Then the bait will shoot out beautifully—if you have timed the operation right. You soon will, after a little practice.

Of course, if you are fishing with only a tiny float and perhaps one solitary split shot on your cast, there is very little weight to pull your line out through the rod rings. In that case you will

46

have to do the best you can swinging out the whole available length of line. But if you are fishing fairly fast water, and therefore using a larger float and a fair amount of shot on the cast, you will find that this will pull the line through the rod rings quite smartly. The main thing is to release the trapped line from your left hand at just the right moment—exactly when the baited hook, flying out, begins to exert a pull on it.

If the cast is properly executed the hook will drop gently into the water and the float will *slide* down into the water after it, with no splash at all. That is as it should be, and it's worth practising for.

Now you have made your first cast, after all this trouble, and you are really fishing. Never fear, all the bother has been well worth while. You have started the right way, the way you mean to go on. Now all we have to do is watch that float as a hawk watches a rat.

(Of course, if you can afford to buy a fixed spool reel you will find it child's play to cast even the lightest bait right across the river. But even now a fixed spool reel costs more than you may want to spend. Anyway, you can find a complete account of how to use the fixed spool reel in Chapter 22.)

7. Fishing the Swim

I AM GOING to assume, now, that you have begun to fish in a river or stream—at any rate in moving water—because if you are fishing in still water there is nothing to do now but wait for a bite, whereas if you have cast into a river there is a great deal to do. Fishing a river is not the idle practice that some people seem to think it when they say to anglers: 'Oh, I don't know how you find the *patience*.' Patience *is* necessary to a good angler, but it is not quite the sort of patience these non-anglers think. Certainly, when you are fishing a river it is not just a matter of sitting down and watching your float.

The usual method of fishing a river is to *fish the swim*. There are several other methods, all useful in the right conditions, and we shall deal with them all later. But fishing a swim is the most usual.

What *is* 'the swim'? The swim is that stretch of water which you have selected as a likely run, and which you can cover comfortably without moving. That is to say, it is a stretch of water a few yards long, extending from slightly upstream of where you sit to some yards downstream. You choose this swim because you like the look of it, you think it will hold fish, and it attracts you personally—all very sound reasons, for you will not fish well if you are not at ease with your surroundings. In the chapters which follow dealing with specific fish, I tell you how to recognize what sort of 'swim' is likely to be the home of fish of various sorts, but the chief characteristic of any swim is that it should be *fishable*. That is to say, there must be an unbroken stretch of a few yards of water *of even depth* down

48

which your baited hook can travel at every cast. If the depth in the swim varies more than a fraction, you will not be able to judge the exact depth at which to fish your bait. For part of the way it will be just right; then the bait will drag along the bottom, pulling your float under and making you think you have a bite; then the bottom will shelve down and your bait will hang far too high in the water. Of course, few swims can be found *perfectly* even in depth all the way, but you must find the best you can, checking the depth over the whole swim, either with your plummet or by trial and error. The very best sort of swim is a level run which *ends*—at the downstream end, that is—in a sudden sharp little depression or shelf. Food drifting along the bottom will tend to collect here, and that includes your ground-bait. Fish love to lie in such holes, which not only provide them with easy feeding but give them some shelter against the force of the current. You see it is well worth while to take the greatest pains to get to know the geography of the river's bed in the area where you plan to fish. Unless you have some notion of what the floor of the river is like, you cannot fish scientifically and you definitely reduce your chances of taking fish.

But having chosen your swim with care and judgment, you now proceed to fish it. Cast your baited hook slightly upstream of where you are sitting and let it travel down the swim until it has passed as far downstream as you can conveniently handle. Watch your float keenly the whole way down, alert for the slightest abnormal movement. When it has reached the end of the swim and shows a tendency to be swung in towards the bank by the force of the current acting on the tight line, raise it very slightly and hold it for a moment against the current. This is the most important moment of the whole swim-down. Often, fish will take the bait at that last moment as it swings up a little from the bottom. Watch for the dip or sideways flicker of the float, ready to strike.

If nothing happens, retrieve your whole cast from the water

as neatly and unobtrusively as you can, making no more disturbance than is essential, and swing the bait back to the upstream end of the swim. *Never* drag it through the water. Always lift it clear and swing it right over to the top again, lowering it into the water silently and craftily. Then swim down again to the far end and repeat the performance.

That is all there is, really, to 'fishing the swim.' But you want to bear in mind two or three subtle little points which make all the difference between a full bag of fish and just one or two small ones.

The first is to sit as far back from the water as you conveniently can. Much depends on the water itself and on the length of your rod, of course; but if there is a chance of fishing out over a patch of reeds, for instance, take it. Another excellent method is to snuggle down on the upstream side of a bush or tree that hangs out over the water. This makes you virtually invisible to fish downstream of you, and by cunningly peering round the trunk of the tree you can keep an eye on your float all the way down the swim.

Secondly, watch the time it takes for your float to cock. If it is not cocking nicely in the very early stages of the swim down, you are wasting too much of your swim. This means that you must cast farther upstream—so that your float is travelling in the right position throughout the baited swim.

Thirdly—*stick it.* There are kinds of fishing in which you are wasting your time if you spend more than a few minutes in one spot—perch and chub fishing, for instance. But if you have chosen a good swim and baited it up with ground-bait, don't give it up just because you get no bites in the first half hour. I know—no one knows better!—the growing sense of disappointment as time ticks by and you haven't had a 'knock.' But if you've gone to all the trouble of baiting-up, and if it is a reasonable swim that you have chosen, then you might just as well stay there as start getting restless. If the fish are feeding at all that day—and there are days when they are *not*—then sooner or later they will start feeding where you have encouraged them to feed by the application of your ground-bait. And if you have stuck it out doggedly, you will reap your rich reward. (This is one of the reasons why I say, choose a swim that attracts you, personally. If you have to spend several fishless hours sitting there, it might as well be a place that you are happy to be in.)

8. Long-corking

'LONG-CORKING' is a lovely word, isn't it? Another name for it is 'long-trotting.' Does it explain itself to you?

What it means is this. Some fish are too shy ever to be caught if you are close to them. They can only be caught if you fish 'fine and far off.' Dace can be caught when you are almost on top of them, if you are quiet—but not big dace. The best dace are caught long-corking. And certainly the best chub. In fact, long-corking is first and foremost a method of catching big, shy chub. But other fish can also be caught, of course, by the use of this curious, difficult, and ingenious method.

The 'cork' in the name, of course, is the float. Long-corking or long-trotting means swimming your float an immense distance downstream—so far downstream that no fish would possibly have an inkling that there was an angler attached in any way to the bait that drifts innocently with the current. It is an absolutely first-rate way of catching big fish.

Obviously, two things are quite essential to long-corking. One is a strongish current. The other is a free-running reel with a lot of line on it.

Another necessity is good eyesight, or a big float, or both. One man who was famous for his long-corking successes used to swim his float down prodigious distances—with a little flag on top of it to keep it in sight.

Well, I expect that your eyes are better than mine, and I can still trot a stream. But you do have to have good eyes, and it is as well to experiment with the colour of your float tip. The conventional colour, I think, is red—and a very jolly, cheerful colour it is. Personally, I find red a difficult colour to see on the water if the light is playing tricks—and it always is: that is one of the beauties of living in this wonderful country. We don't have very many of those blazing, boring days of hard sunlight. Most days the light is infinitely variable, with cunning fluctuations of cloud formation. The bottom of the river is always changing colour too, and all these variations mean that a float tip which is plainly visible at one moment is in shadow at the next. So use the colour which you find suits your eyes best. I like yellow—a rather deep, ochre-ish yellow—which I find stands out well against any surface shade. But some people find white best, and there is one school of thought which holds that a black tip is the easiest to pick out in conditions of tricky light. Incidentally, while we are on the subject, the underside of your float—the part which is submerged—*must not* be painted a bright colour. Too many are. Red or vivid green is quite common. But the submerged part of the float, though practically invisible, perhaps, to you, actually reflects a surprising amount of light from the *bottom* of the water. A fish will see the flash of a vivid float and be put off. Always paint the bottom part of your float a drab, greenish-olive or grey colour.

Well, here is the technique of long-corking. You have to take a chance on variations in the depth of the river, for obviously you cannot plumb the depth along a stretch that may extend for anything from 50 to 100 yards (according to how much line your reel will hold and how strong the current is). You set your float at what you think a reasonably safe depth—within a few inches of the bottom—and you cast out your float into mid-stream—or into the strongest current, which may not be mid-stream, of course. (You can always test the current, if your eyes are not yet accustomed to judging water, by tossing a few bits of twig on the surface and watching them travel.)

Now pay out line. This again is far easier said than done. Indeed, it is the whole art of long-corking. Reels *do* exist—I am lucky enough to own one, an Allcock's 'Aerial'—which are so easy-running that the mere pressure of the current on the float will draw line off the reel at the required rate. Long-corking with such a reel is child's play. But not all reels are so beautifully balanced. Generally you have to pull line off the reel yourself, and let the current draw merely the weight of that bit of line through the rings of the rod.

Keep your rod tip low and pointing in the direction of the float, so that the whole outfit is as nearly as possible in a straight line. Holding the rod firmly with the right hand, draw off a few inches of line at a time with your left hand. Practice is needed to make sure that you do not pull off such a big loop that the float cannot pull it downstream fast enough, and it hangs uselessly fouling the rod rings. After all, you want to keep the line reasonably taut from reel to float—otherwise, even if you do get a bite, you will never hook the fish. On the other hand, unless you keep paying out line fast enough to keep up with the float's speed down the current, the float will be checked every few moments. This is the very last thing you want. The whole point of long-corking is to keep a bait dribbling down the river *at the natural speed of the current*, so that any fish seeing it will have no suspicion that there is anything crooked going on.

What makes it worse, if you pay out line in jerks instead of evenly, is that the float is always being checked in its trot downstream, the baited hook will rise in a foolish manner from the bed of the stream and hang in mid water. No fair-sized fish is fool enough to be deceived by *that*.

It's just a matter of practice, like almost everything else. With a good strongish current, a fairly clean bed to the river, and a steady hand on the reel, you can trot amazing distances downstream. But there is just one thing that is absolutely essential to success—without it you might as well pack up and gather daisies. That is: *the line must float perfectly*. Not fairly well, not in parts, but perfectly. If it becomes drowned, you will never make a successful strike, and the farther away your bait travels the less chance you will have of hooking a fish. So take the trouble to grease your line really thoroughly—long before you start fishing. The best way is to tie one end to a fence and walk backwards until all the reel line is extended. Then go over it thoroughly with Mucilin, rubbing it well in with your fingers. A line so treated will float throughout a long, hard day. (You should always aim at a perfectly floating line, whether you are going to try long-corking or not.) Remember that a thin line will float much better than a thick one.

You will wonder what depth is best for trotting. Well, the lower the bait travels the better you are likely to do, by and large. But there is another point to consider, which has a bearing on this problem. It is far better for your bait to precede the float than the other way round. If your bait is dragging on the bottom the float will naturally swim on ahead, hauling the reluctant bait along behind it. You are not so likely to catch fish this way. You see why, don't you? For one thing, an inquisitive fish is more likely to notice the taut piece of nylon which is hauling the reluctant bait along. For another, since there will be a great bulge or angle in the line, you will find it unnecessarily difficult to hook your fish when he does bite.

Hooking is hard enough, when you are long-trotting. Your float is way downstream, perhaps scores of yards, when it goes under. Under the best of circumstances there will be lots of slack line between you and the hook. The only thing to do when the float disappears is to swing back the whole rod in an almighty great swipe. The strike when long-corking is the *only* strike in all float fishing which must be really vigorous, whole-hearted, and big. Lay that rod back with a will. Remember it has to take up all the slack that has developed in your line and, furthermore, it has to cut the line through a lot of water, which offers a surprising resistance. So go to it with a will.

As I said, you need a good stream to carry your float down.

But it doesn't have to be a raging torrent. Fishing in a raging torrent is waste of time anyway, for fish just do not like raging torrents. Most fish are bone-idle, and they are not going to spend their energy fighting a powerful current if there is an easier way of getting a meal. Your ideal stream for long-corking is a good, steady, moderate current which will keep your float moving *slowly*. If when you trap the line against the rod with a finger your float lies flat and you feel a *gentle* tug at the top of the rod, that is a nice stream for trotting.

It is a simply wonderful way of catching fish, and you must try it one day. There is no bother about ground-baiting—whch would be worse than useless in such conditions. You fix up a big float which will carry a lot of weight, put on a big hook and a whacking great knob of bread-paste or cheese—or, of course, a bunch of maggots or a lob worm if you like—and send it off on its voyage of exploration. The fascination of this sort of fishing is that it always seems to attract the bigger fish—if it is properly done. If the line is paid out smoothly and evenly.

There is a sort of compromise long-corking which you might like to try out first, before you try your hand at the really long trips. Bait up a good spot—preferably one under a bush or tree that hangs over the water, and which is difficult to fish in the ordinary way. Give it a real good baiting-up, day after day for several days if you can. If you can't, just drop in a nice handful of ground-bait at the start of the day's fishing, then go away and fish elsewhere for an hour or so. But come back to that spot.

Well, not exactly. But bring a baited hook back to it. Station yourself about fifteen to twenty yards upstream of your baited spot, and let your float drift quietly down, paying out line as I've told you how, until it reaches the baited hole. Almost certainly you will find that you have to swim your float down the main current—but if you have chosen a good spot to bait that will be rather *out* of the main current. Well, then, let your float run down until it is opposite the baited hole, and then check the line. The float will swing in towards the bank and will present your bait to the fish which is (we hope, and with reason) grubbing about among your ground-bait. This is my own patent method and has accounted for lots of fine fish, not only chub but roach, good dace, and a perch or two. I make you a present of it.

I am very fond of this little ruse. You see, it combines the advantages of ground-baiting and long-corking. Long-corking alone is terribly exciting and sometimes very rewarding—but owing to the impossibility of ground-baiting over such distances, it *is* slightly hit-and-miss, let us face it. It depends on the fish happening to be just there when your bait arrives. Whereas my method makes sure that the fish *will* be there when your bait arrives.

Oh dear, I ought not to have said that! Never, never, never is there such a thing as certainty in angling. Thank goodness. It would be a fairly dull business if we could be *sure* of catching fish. What I should have said, of course, is that my method makes it a good deal more likely that when your bait arrives innocently at the appointed spot, some fish, attracted by the ground-bait, will be ready to give it a hearty welcome.

The best days for long-corking, in my experience, are winter days when the river is good and clear but not either too high or too low. When a river is fining down after a flood is always a good time to try a bit of long-corking—for that matter, it is a good time to try any sort of fishing.

9. Ledgering, Float-ledgering, and Laying-on

ANOTHER NICE bunch of words, aren't they? The fisherman acquires a glorious vocabulary, unintelligible to non-anglers.

No one is likely to tell you the origin of the term 'ledgering': at least, I have asked the question in the columns of a distinguished newspaper that is read by some of the most learned scholars in the country, and they could not tell me. One idea is that the word comes from the old Anglo-Saxon word *leggen*, which means 'to lay' or 'to lie.' Certainly it has nothing to do with account books.

But who cares for the derivation of a word when there is the chance of using this method actually at the waterside? Not that it is, by any means, my idea of thrilling fishing. In fact, it is one of the very few ways of fishing which can be rather dull. But—and it is a very big but—ledgering accounts for some of the very biggest fish, season after season. So we cannot ignore it.

In a word, ledgering means letting your bait rest solidly on the bottom of the water until a fish picks it up and eats it. No float is used—you just watch your line, or the tip of your rod. That is why it can be rather dull when fish are not biting.

But it has some obvious advantages. It enables you to get the bait right down on the bottom, and to leave it there for as long as you like. This means a lot when you are dealing with particularly cunning fish—and all fish that have grown to a good age and a good size are pretty cunning.

Another very real advantage of ledgering is that you can so arrange matters that the most suspicious fish will not feel the slight resistance which a float naturally offers, and will therefore take a bait which he would otherwise drop as soon as he felt the unnatural weight of the float. Finally, with a ledger you can really reach out easily to water that you might not be able to reach with a float.

Ledger tackle consists of a hefty weight with a hole drilled through it. That is all. That is the heart of the matter. You can buy this weight in any of several fancy shapes and sizes: it doesn't really matter twopence. There is the coffin-shaped lead, the drilled bullet (round, of course), and the long oval lead. Perhaps the coffin lead is very slightly better than the others because it does not so easily get sunk in the mud on the bottom, nor does it roll along in a current.

You pass your cast through the ledger lead, attach the hook-length, and nip on one small split shot on the hook side of the ledger, about two feet away from the hook itself. This split shot prevents the ledger from sliding right down to the hook—but it does not prevent a fish from drawing line through the ledger. The illustration (Figure 4) makes all clear. I want to mention that if you think this drawing is out of proportion, you're quite right. It is meant to be—to show up the 'business end' of the tackle.

You mould a big lump of ground-bait round the ledger itself, bait your hook, and heave the whole thing out into the water. Very gently and carefully, reel in line until the line runs fairly straight from rod-tip to water: almost taut. Put your rod down, resting it in a Y-shaped stick driven into the ground. Pinch a scrap of bread-paste, or tie a feather, on the line just where it leaves the tip of the rod. This will serve as your tell-tale—the indicator of a bite. Some anglers carefully pull a few feet of line off the reel and coil it on a piece of paper, or a groundsheet. Their only indication of a bite is when this coil of line begins to slide away.

Well, frankly, that is all there is, basically, to the old practice of ledgering. The big weight keeps your bait in one spot. The

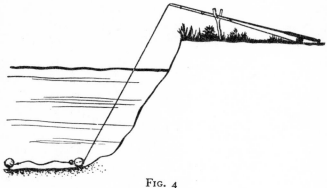

FIG. 4

absence of a float, or of any weights on the line (apart from that one tiny split shot) means that even a suspicious fish may take the bait without a care in the world. It certainly works wonderfully well. But it isn't my idea of brighter fishing.

But even I will admit that there are circumstances in which the ledger really comes into its own. When you are faced by a stream so strong that it is almost impossible to fish the swim comfortably, the ledger is the job. In very fast water it is the *only* way of getting the bait down to the bottom and holding it there. Yes, it pays.

There are variations of the ledgering technique, but mighty half-hearted ones, which I personally do not greatly like. (I don't like anything half-hearted. Wilfred Pickles's famous motto seems to me to sum up a very good way to look at life: '*Have a go, Joe.*' Have a go, right or wrong: living and learning to your dying day.)

One variation is called 'float-ledgering.' This is a rum sort of compromise. You have a float on your line, but instead of using just enough split shot to cock it you use the pierced bullet of

Common Carp

Perch

Roach

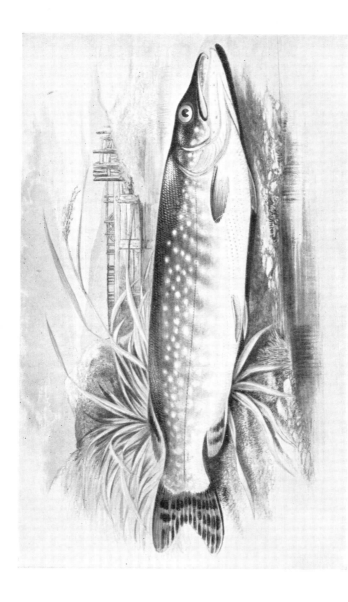

Pike

Chub

Dace

Common Bream

Brown Trout

the true ledger. You estimate the depth of the water at the point where your baited hook will lie, and have your float at slightly more than that distance away from the hook. Thus, when you cast, your bait lies securely anchored on the bottom, but your float, approximately half-cocked, still serves to warn you in the usual way of a bite.

No doubt this method was evolved by fishermen who, like me, find watching a ledger-line slightly dull. But it seems to me to combine the worst of both systems without the virtues of either. It means that you still have the not inconsiderable weight of the float on the line, and a really astute fish will feel it. And it robs you of the real charm and utility of the float, which is the freedom it bestows on the angler to fish down a stream. However, this system is much used, and in rather fast streamy water it *does* work.

The second variation—a frightful cross between ledgering and float-ledgering—is called laying-on. This simply means using ordinary float tackle (no ledger bullet) but having a distance between float and hook quite considerably greater than the distance between the surface and the bottom of the water. The result is that your float, instead of cocking, leans drunkenly over at an acute angle. To make this method workable you need to keep a fairly tightish line between rod-tip and float. I can see no virtues in this method, and hardly ever use it. The fish is bound to feel the weight of all, or almost all, the shots on the line the moment he mouths the bait. A truly cocked float is felt hardly at all, for all its weight is suspended in the water, and it glides under without setting up much resistance. But the fish that takes the bait of a layer-on must not only actually lift up the split shot that are lying on the bottom, but must then—if he isn't already scared off—drag under water a float which is lying flat, and therefore offering maximum resistance. I know that many fish are caught while laying-on, but contend that more—or, rather, *better*—fish are caught by other methods. I tell you about it only because it is a fairly common method of fishing, and you must know all the available techniques in order that you may form your own opinion.

When you know all the accepted ways of angling, you will no doubt find one or two methods particularly appealing to you. They will suit your own particular temperament. Well, those are the methods for you. I wouldn't dream of trying to persuade you that there was only one way of catching fish—my way. Not at all. You may find laying-on suits you very well. It is certainly an easy, even a lazy way of fishing, and sometimes I have reverted to it when I have grown tired of fishing the swim or trotting, and feel too lazy to change my tackle and do a bit of genuine ledgering. Nevertheless, I have felt it a duty not only to explain this method to you but to hand on my personal opinion that true ledgering is far more deadly. Indeed, I would hazard a guess that long-corking and true ledgering are responsible for the capture of more *big* fish than any other methods.

I should add that some of the real experts never lay their rod in a rest, even when ledgering. They hold it all the time. True, this gives you greater control and a better chance of hitting a bite. I suppose it all depends on how keen you are, and how lazy—and, of course, it depends a bit on how steady your hand is. It *must* be steady, for if it trembles you will certainly frighten off the fish.

10. Paternostering

'PATERNOSTER' is another word which no one has ever explained to me. I guess that it may possibly have been inspired by the monks who used to keep fish—mainly carp, perhaps—in their stewponds and catch them every Thursday to eat every Friday. But that is a wild guess.

Anyway, the paternoster is a curious bit of tackle which can be deadly at times and in certain circumstances. The picture explains it perfectly (Figure 5). You see that, unlike a ledger, the paternoster aims to keep the bait well off the bottom, while anchoring the whole outfit to one spot.

A paternoster can have one swivelling boom, as shown in our illustration, or two, or (theoretically) any number, ranged above one another at varying heights. I am against having more than one, for the more you multiply the machinery of your tackle the more likely are the fish to see all the machinery and sheer off, puzzled and suspicious.

The usefulness of a paternoster is that when the bottom is muddy, soft, or carpeted with slushy dead leaves, you can keep your bait well above the slush. A risk you always take when ledgering is that your bait may have sunk out of sight. The paternoster cuts out that risk. It is true, of course, as you will learn from the chapters on various fish, that not every fish feeds on the bottom. Some—notably roving perch—feed freely in mid water. The paternoster enables you to present a bait at any depth you like—and unlike a travelling bait, it will stay put just where you want it to.

But the snag of the paternoster to my mind is that it is only

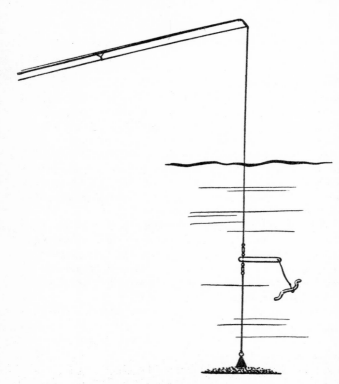

FIG. 5

really suitable for live baits. Indeed, that is what it is generally used for. Among live baits I include worms, as you know. A paternoster baited with a minnow or a lively worm can work havoc among perch, and even pike. And it has another great advantage. Whatever the state of the water, you can jog along the bank with your paternoster already rigged up and drop it quietly into every likely looking hole and corner, every promising bay and eddy. I cannot deny the great utility of a paternoster. But it is not so useful for the baits I like to use, such as paste and bread and cheese—for a lump of bread hanging in mid water must look odd to any fish. However, it anchors live-bait very efficiently. The wretched minnow swims round and round, unable to bolt for cover as a live-bait may on ordinary snap-tackle, and if a perch or pike takes a fancy to him, there is no escaping. Yes, a deadly tackle for the live-baiter, a useful tackle for the worm fisher. No use to me at all. Again, I tell you about it because I want you to know all there is to know about current techniques. That doesn't make me like it.

11. Detecting Bites

EVERYBODY KNOWS that if the float disappears you might as well haul away, for the likely explanation is that a fish has dragged it under. Ah! if only 'twere as simple as all that! The fact is that there are all sorts of bites, an almost infinite number of different bites, and he is a good angler who can identify them all, interpret the varying quavers and dips and skips and tremors, and who knows just by looking at the float exactly what is going on under water.

That is what we must all aim to do, of course. That is what the float is for—to tell us what is happening under water, out of sight. The float speaks a thrilling, strange, mysterious language of its own, which we must learn to translate as we go along.

Now in those long-promised chapters on individual fish— yes, they really are coming: they start right away after this chapter—in them I tell you as best I can just how different sorts of fish register their interest in your bait. You will soon learn to tell the difference between the faint tremble of a cautious roach, the bob-o-bob of a perch, the tug of a gudgeon, the slashing dive of a chub, the lightning oblique dip of a dace, and so on. Some bites you can't 'hit' too fast: others you must give ample time to develop. But one thing holds good whatever fish you are angling for. It's not a bit of good identifying the bite unless you hook the fish.

The longer I live the more I am inclined to believe that more fish are lost through bad striking than for any other reason— with the sole exception of the approach, about which I wrote at some length in the earlier part of this book. Even if your approach has been a model of caution, even if your handling of the tackle is flawless, your judgment of the water excellent, your bait delicious—even then you will not have fish on the bank unless you hook them properly.

Now 'striking,' as it is called, is intensely difficult to argue about. It should not be called striking at all: it should be called *hooking*. The word strike gives an altogether false impression. You hook your fish, if you are going to hook him at all, with the neatest, smallest, sharpest motion imaginable. Only when long-corking, as I have explained, do you need to give a really hefty heave, and the reasons for that are obvious enough.

I shall never forget the first little roach I caught. The first fish I caught were perch, which are very easy indeed to catch if they are there to be caught. I soon decided I must catch roach as well, and fished for hours, with bite after bite, before I hooked one. When I *did* hook it I gave so prodigious a heave that the poor little fish went flying up in the air, over my shoulder, and landed behind me in a hawthorn bush.

Now that is just how not to do it. Not only is a huge 'strike' quite unnecessary to hook a small fish—but, what is more to the point, such a strike would certainly result in smashed tackle if the fish happened to be a good one. You can heave little roach clean out of the water even on the finest of tackle. Big ones stay put, and the tackle has to give way. I cannot begin to compute the number of times I have been 'smashed up' in my early days. I used to like to kid myself that it was always a big fish that broke me, but the truth is that I broke myself by wild swiping.

Of course, you can overdo it and strike so softly and slowly that the fish is away with the bait, laughing, long before you set the hook moving. Some fish hook themselves, sometimes; not very often. Most fish will have the bait off the hook and be yards away, digesting it, before you can do anything about it—unless you cultivate that snappy wrist movement which moves the hook upwards *with speed but without too much force*. Make your motto *fast but not ferocious*. It all stems from a good co-ordination of eye and hand. The crack match angler is striking almost before his eye has told him that a bite is developing—just that smart upwards and sideways turn of the wrist does the trick.

Of course, some rods make it easy to hook fish, some make it hard. A perfect 'roach rod' is stiff for three-quarters of its length, quite rigid, although light. All its 'action' is concentrated in a yard or so of thin, tempered built-cane (or fibre glass) at the tip. This means that a fisherman can get a tremendously speedy upward movement of the tip without any movement of the butt to speak of. A softer-actioned rod will be slower in the strike. Such a rod as an old greenheart fly-rod, for example, is, roughly speaking, more or less even in its action throughout its whole length. It follows, then, that for a given upward movement of the tip you must apply an almost equal movement of the butt. You must really *swing* a soft rod up, quite hard and fast, to produce quite a small upward movement of the tip itself. And a soft rod, of course, presents another problem. When you raise such a rod, even sharply, the tip will actually dip down before it begins to spring up. Hold any rod out and try it. If you hold it horizontally over a table and strike smartly, you will hear the tip rap on the table before it springs upwards. Now this characteristic of a rod means delay in the actual upward movement of the hook, and you must make allowance for it in your fishing. (*All* rods suffer from this dip to some extent, so don't worry about it. Just learn how slow or how fast your rod's tip is, and fish accordingly.)

I will go so far as to say that I think it a very good thing to start your fishing career with a soft-actioned rod, even quite a whippy one. You will develop real speed in striking which will stand you in very good stead when you come to use a genuine roach rod, or 'match' rod, with its Spanish reed body and lightning tip. Yes, if I were giving a boy his first-ever rod (and my goodness, how often I *have*!) it would for preference be an old greenheart trout fly rod. Then when he progresses to float fishing with a super rod, he also owns a rod that will do beautifully for fly-fishing!

There is another very important point about this hooking business. The shrewd angler always has his left hand on the line. Most anglers who know the game hold the line just above the reel, between the first finger and thumb of the left hand. (If you are long-corking, of course, you are bound to have the line passing through the first finger and thumb of the left hand, all the time as you strip off line.) This means that you can double the speed of the strike—by pulling the line in fast and hard with the left hand at the same time that you raise the rod tip with the right hand. Never just hold the rod in the right hand; always make a two-handed job of it, keeping direct contact with the line with your left hand. (Left-handed anglers will do the opposite, of course: that is understood.) This habit will stand you in good stead when you graduate to fly-fishing, as I sincerely hope you will.

One thing you must *not* do is to trap the line against the rod with any finger. If you do this, it means that you have given up the value of the reel and are fishing virtually with a 'tight line.' For the actual instant of hooking that does not matter in the least, but it is the *next* instant that matters. You will hook the fish solidly, no doubt—but after a split-second pause to get his breath back, that fish is going to *move*. Like lightning. And unless you are rather lucky, you will be too slow releasing the line; and the fish—if he is a good one—may break you.

No. Keep the line between the first finger and thumb of your left hand, and hold the rod comfortably at the point of balance in your right. Strike by making the smart double movement— left hand out, right hand up—and the moment you feel the fish is 'on,' ease the grip of the left hand on the line and prepare to hear the reel sing. Needless to say, it may only be a little fish after all—but always, always, *always* be on the alert for the big one. Carelessness is what saves the lives of innumerable big fish. Not their carelessness; the fisherman's.

I tell you just how various fish bite and play in the chapters immediately following this one. But there is a general rule about 'playing' fish. It surprises me how many people, even adult anglers of much experience, forget it in the heat of battle. It is, simply: *Keep your rod tip up*. After all, it is the spring, the elasticity, of your rod which cushions the plunges of the fish— if you had a rigid rod you would be broken every time you hooked a good fish, unless your line were like rope. The elasticity of your rod makes it possible to land good fish on fine tackle —but you must let the rod work. If you drop the tip of the rod towards the fish, as so many beginners do, you are in effect playing the hand on a handline—your line runs almost straight from reel to fish—and you have given up the safety margin which the springiness of the rod represents. So keep the rod well up—an angle of forty-five degrees is just about right—and let it do its proper work. A fish will tire pretty fast if every plunge he makes just bends a rod that springs upright again the moment he relaxes.

Mark you, you can hold the rod right down parallel with the water if you like—provided that you *keep an acute angle between rod and line*. Ninety degrees or less—anything between that and forty-five degrees is a really efficient angle, which means quick defeat for the fish and safety for you.

In a real emergency, if you hook a monster which you cannot handle, or if your reel jams, or something horrible and probable like that, there is a tip worth remembering. Thrust the rod tip under water. Then the infinitely variable pressure of the water is added to the resilience of the rod, and you may well come out the victor. If you are beaten all ends up and feel sure he is going to smash you any second, throw your rod into the water. Towing that around won't suit the fish. It's long odds you will get it back again, when you've got your breath and worked out a plan of campaign, with the beaten fish—if it was well hooked —still on the line and as meek as a lamb.

If you are playing a fish normally, by the reel, take care that you don't get surprised by a sudden dash of the fish. A strong fish of good fighting heart—a perch, say—is often capable of a terrific last-minute burst just when you think you have him safely cooked. If this last-second rush catches you with your fingers neatly snarled all round the reel handles so that you can't give line instantly, you risk a break. Always keep the body of your hand arched away from the reel, and only your first finger and thumb actually touching the reel handle. Be ready for that mad rush for freedom—ready to give line. And don't panic in those awe-inspiring moments—the last rush means a soon-to-be-beaten and docile fish.

Always try to play a fish deep down. There is an irresistible temptation, I know, to haul him up to the surface and have a look at him. Resist it. A fish playing on the surface is a lot more dangerous than a fish playing deep. As he jumps and threshes around, his *real* weight is varying all the time, according to how much of his mass is being supported by the water and how much in the air, is being wholly supported by your line. You can't afford to take such risks with a good fish.

And there is another point, perhaps even more important—a fish splashing on the surface causes a great deal of disturbance and may well put his pals wise to the fact that something very sinister is going on. Whereas a fish playing deep will not alarm its fellows one bit. Time and again I have watched a hooked fish playing in deepish, clear water. The other fish seem mildly surprised at his antics, and sometimes one or two of them will swim round with him, keeping him company as he dives and rolls and plunges, and obviously wondering what has got into him to make him behave so oddly. They do not seem to take much notice of his eventual departure to a better land. But a fish wallowing and splashing on the surface is another matter. Try to tire him out without pulling him up. When he comes up of his own accord, he's nearly beaten.

I don't suppose you own a landing-net. I didn't recommend you to buy or beg one, because you have enough to buy to be going on with. Undeniably they are very useful things. I hardly ever use one myself, and my fishing friends call me reckless. True, I lose a fish now and then, but what's a lost fish? I would rather lose a third of all the fish I hook than have the fearful bother of carrying a landing-net. Mark you, I'm really more of a rover than a sit-down angler: spinning and fly-fishing are my favourite pursuits. And I don't like being cluttered up with gear: 'travel light through life' is another maxim which appeals to me. Travel light, don't burden yourself with possessions you don't really need and which drag you down to a crawl.

If you do have a landing-net, well, it's fairly simple to land a fish. Just remember one or two little points. *Sink the net and draw the fish over it.* That's the golden rule. Don't make stabs at the fish with the net. Don't be in too much of a hurry. Play the fish out and draw him gently over the submerged net. The moment he's safely over the rim, up with the net in one swift, smooth movement—and turn away from the water. Fish are mighty scared by nets, and have been known to jump out! In fact, it is a dangerous moment when the fish touches the net's rim. That's why I say, play him right out until he's lying inert on his side on the surface.

Some people, I notice, have plenty of trouble through reeling in too much line. I don't know if you remember any trigonometry, but if you do, you won't need me to explain that if the distance from rod-tip to fish is too short, you won't be able to reach the fish with the net. You just won't. So don't reel in too much. Draw the fish gently to the water at your feet *with the rod held very high.* Then that last desperate thrashing of the fish will not catch you unprepared. It will be absorbed by the rod, whereas otherwise it could easily smash your cast. There is little doubt in my mind that the most dangerous moments when playing a fish are the first instant after hooking and the last instant before netting.

I never like to prolong the playing of a fish one moment longer than is absolutely necessary. But you just can't hustle a strong fish to the net on fine tackle. If he is determined to run, you must let him run. But never let him run unchecked. You need to judge just how much pressure you can safely put on a running fish without risking a break. Some anglers have fine hands—'hands' in the sense that a horseman is said to have 'hands'—but some are incurably ham-fisted.

The check of your reel will do a lot of work for you, if you choose just to let a fish pull against the ratchet. It may seem to you that the ratchet imposes practically no strain, but in fact the effort of pulling line off a reel against the check will very soon tire a fish. A strain of half a pound, maintained unremittingly for a few minutes, will take the fight out of quite a good fish. With certain noble exceptions—salmon, barbel, carp, for instance— fish do not have great *reserves* of energy, and though they can move fast for a short time they are mainly sprinters, not stayers.

The greatest mistake you can make when playing a fish is to let the line go slack. This is the fish's chance to get rid of the hook. If a fish is only lightly hooked, as often happens, the hook will drop out the moment the line goes slack. This is one danger, but there is another. If the line is allowed to go slack, then in the nature of things it must tighten up again some time—and it is ten to one that it will tighten up with a jerk. And a jerk is the one thing you must always guard against when you are fishing. Even very fine gut or nylon will stand a surprising strain, if that strain is steadily applied. But a sudden snatch will break it. So seek always to maintain that steady, killing pressure. I always take what my friends call fantastic risks when playing a fish. I don't much like the business of playing, and want to get it over. I haul away, and the fish hauls away, and quite often one of us has a nasty surprise. Sometimes it's me, I admit; oftener it's Fred Fish. (But though I take risks with the pressure I put on the nylon, I never take risks with the knots I tie in it. Nylon is champion stuff, don't let anyone tell you it isn't: but you *do* have to watch the knots, especially in the finer gauges.)

73

Now for landing a fish without a landing-net. You must tail him. Tailing means picking a fish out of the water by grasping him near the tail. It appears to be a quite nerve-racking business, and most of my fishing friends dislike it intensely. But it's as safe as houses, if you don't lose your nerve.

There are two important points to remember about tailing a fish. Firstly, your thumb and fingers must point to the fish's tail, not to his head. You put your hand down over the fish in the shape of a V, and the point of that V must be towards the head of the fish. Then when the fish feels you and squirms forward, the great swelling of his tail will come up solid against the point of the V, and the harder he pushes himself forward the more firmly he will lock himself against your hand. If you do it the other way round, with the point of the V towards the tail, the fish will slip out like grease.

Secondly, your hand will get a better grip if it is covered by linen or cotton. How on earth? Well, some intrepid anglers drop a handkerchief over the fish and grab that. You may find the handkerchief floating away downstream and the fish dashing upstream. I use a cotton glove of the sort used by ladies when doing the chores—I think it is probably called a 'household' glove. They are loose-fitting and inexpensive, made of some sort of cheap cotton. Of course, I don't wear it all the time— indeed, I never wear gloves, winter or summer, and no angler should. Get your hands hardened to the weather and they will be a lot more use to you in your fishing. I carry my left-handed glove tucked lightly into my left-hand coat pocket, with the open wrist part peeping out. When I guess the fish is ready to be picked out, I plunge my left hand into this and wriggle the glove on, using my teeth if necessary to pull it right on. Then I stoop down—holding the rod up in the right hand, of course—and pick the fish out as neat as a heron. It saves a lot of bother.

I think that's all about getting a fish ashore.

PART III:
STILL WATER AND STREAM

~~~~~~

12. The Choice

~~~~~~

ALL FISHING is fun, but sooner or later you inevitably come to have preferences. Some anglers, once they have discovered the delights of fly-fishing for trout or salmon, give up every other sort of fishing. (And what is worse, come rather to despise it. This is very foolish.) Some settle for spinning, which is one of the most popular, and certainly one of the most interesting, ways of catching fish. But there is another distinction, and that is the distinction between fishing still water and fishing running water. Many and many an angler, after trying both, begins to feel that the one or the other attracts him most keenly, and gradually he settles down into a one-style fisherman. There is no doubt that if you want a bit of activity to keep you interested, running water will attract you most. But if you like just to sit quite still and watch a float, then still-water fishing is the fishing for you.

Personally, I prefer rivers to lakes, and would rather rove a river's bank casting a spinning bait or a fly than sit on the bank fishing with a float. I still love float fishing, but when I am float fishing I like best to settle down by still water and really relax. Without a shadow of doubt, fishing a lake or pool with a float or ledger is *the* most relaxing, the easiest, and the most restful sort of fishing there is.

When I say still-water fishing is easier, I don't mean that it is so easy that it lacks interest. Far from it. You must be quite cunning to lure fair-sized fish from still water. But provided you go about it the right way, you can catch fish from still water with less expenditure of energy than from running water. You are not always on the move, nor are you constantly shifting your tackle and casting it again (not if you are wise, that is).

I am always in love with rivers; the movement and murmur of running water is an enchantment that never fails. But there is something about large, still sheets of water, brooding, silent, and mysterious, which is terribly attractive, and I expect you too will find it so. Fishing the lake, you take your ease in a setting that was surely designed by God to bring peace to the troubled mind. By the time the float begins to tremble and you are suddenly startled into full alertness, you have already made your peace with the world and are ready for the adventure of the unseen depths.

13. Fish That Live in Still and Running Water

PIKE, OF COURSE, inhabit both still and running water: but since pike-fishing is a sport all on its own, which is dealt with in a later chapter, we will ignore them just now.

The ROACH is almost certainly the most popular fish in Britain. It is the sparrow of the water. It is found in most parts of the country; but not, I understand, in the north of Scotland. I am sure that there are more roach fishers than any other sort, which is hardly surprising, since you find the roach in almost every water. And a nice fish it is too: a little bit sheepish, I suppose, and not what you would call a tough guy among fish: nevertheless a very beautiful fish that gives sport to an immense number of anglers who don't ask very much.

I should get just a little bit tired of roaching, myself, if there were nothing else to fish for. A roach of ordinary size is a bit too easy to catch for my liking, and he gives up the struggle a bit too feebly. On the other hand, *big* roach are terribly difficult to catch; there is no fish shyer. If ever you are lucky or clever enough to land a two-pound roach, you can give yourself the airs of a county cricketer: the number of men who have honestly landed two-pound roach is probably smaller than the number of county cricketers. Yes, probably much smaller. I never have, though I have come desperately near the magic mark.

Having rather libelled the roach in those remarks, I must admit that in the depths of winter the roach is a different proposition from the feeble sluggard of high summer. You can actually feel him struggling.

And there is another amend which I must now make to the

host of extremely skilful roach fishers of the north of England. These men are absolute dab hands: they use gut as fine, even, as 10X, which is approximately as fine as a cobweb. And on this gossamer tackle the handling even of a sheepish old roach is a task that calls for very fine hands. I would not want to libel these brilliant roach fishers, who lure roach out of still, clear water with tackle that I would not willingly use to sew on a button.

No, there are brilliant roach fishers as there are brilliant trout fishers. All I say is that I would not willingly give my life to roach fishing so long as I could find any other sort of fish. But every man to his taste: some people find it just their cup of tea, and good luck to them. Roach are quite good to eat, I will admit.

The main characteristic of roach fishing is the very puzzling *bite*. Roach that inhabit fast, deep rivers bite sharply and clearly enough, but these are heavily outnumbered by the roach that inhabit placid, gently flowing waters and still waters. And the bite of a roach in gentle water can be a puzzler.

It varies. You have to learn a lot of bites off by heart to say that you know a roach when you see his bite. Remember that the roach is timid: he does not often make a determined grab at the bait and pluck your float neatly out of sight. His main aim is to suck at the bait without committing himself one way or another. So what you often see is a faint trembling of the float tip—just a sort of shiver or shudder, hardly perceptible to the unpractised eye. Indeed, more often than not you do not actually see the float move, but you do see a little ring spreading around the float tip, fading away into the stillness of the surrounding water. *This is a bite*. Strike when you see that ring, that tremor— or it will be too late. A roach which is tackling your bait as suspiciously as that is never going to take the float right under. In a moment he will have the bait off the hook, and if you sit waiting you will never know that all you have to entice a fish is a bit of bare, curved, fanged wire.

Another indication is a slight *sideways* movement of the float. *This is a bite.*

Yet another way of losing a roach is to fail to strike when the float *rises* slightly. *This is a bite.*

The point about roach bites, you see, is that they are often over before you notice them. A roach *does* sometimes take the float right under, of course—but you mustn't sit waiting until that happens, or all you will catch is immature little fish hardly worth catching. A roach bite does not have a beginning, a middle, and an end, like some other sorts of bite. It never develops. It is over and done with in a flash, literally in a flash. Speed, a very sharp eye, and knowledge of how the fish behaves are essential if you are to hook fair-sized roach in slow or still water.

Generally speaking, fine tackle is necessary to deceive good roach. The slower and clearer the water, the finer the tackle. Without going to the extreme of the brilliant roach fishers of the north and east of England, you must have a hook-length which is as near invisible as your hands will cope with: say, 6X. It follows that your 'strike' must be sharp but short—the moment the hook has entered, you must be very careful not to pull too hard. Of course, in faster rivers, where you have to float your bait a long way downstream to the fish, you must use rather stouter tackle and strike much harder to pick up all that line off the water and tighten the hook home.

It goes without saying, I hope, that fine hook-tackle means correspondingly fine tackle everywhere else. Always try to make your whole outfit *balance*. You will not want a heavy, big float and dozens of split shot when you are using a fine hook-length and a small hook. (You need a small hook for roach, by the way. Size 12 should be the maximum, and 14 is better.) Nor do you want a heavy, stiff rod, which will smash your tackle more certainly than the fish will. The ideal tackle for roach fishing in clear, still water is a tiny float of the sort called a 'toothpick'—

because that is what it most resembles—a 14 or 16 hook to a yard length of really fine nylon, one shot pinched on the cast just below the float, and a stiffish rod with all the action concentrated in a slender, quick-action tip.

The idea of having the weight immediately below the float is to let the actual baited hook drift down slowly through the water under its own weight. A split shot would sink it faster than is natural—and sharp-eyed timorous roaches will notice something unnatural about such a thing. Some fishers merely wrap a turn of lead wire around the bottom of the float itself— just enough to make it cock properly.

Generally speaking, roach take their food right on the bottom. You will find it pays to have your bait actually dragging on the bottom, then. But there are sometimes exceptions. I don't know why, but occasionally roach may be taken in mid water. So if you are having no luck at all, do not give up until you have tried sliding your float progressively down towards the hook, a couple of inches at a time.

The ideal ground-bait for roach is that cloud which we discussed earlier. You moisten a little at the waterside, forming a loose lump in your hand, and toss it in just where your float is going. Then, as it sinks, in goes your bait after it, sinking through this attractive-looking cloud of tiny food particles. *But*—and you have to remember this constantly—there is more than half a chance that a roach, investigating the delightful cloud, will come upon your baited hook as it is still travelling slowly downwards. This will result in one of those bites which call for real alertness if you are to hook your fish. It might be the merest sideways movement, it might be just the faintest tremble. *Strike* and be sure.

Standard baits for roach: bread-paste (small knobs—though if you are troubled by tiddlers, try a huge lump, the size of a big hazel nut, for a change, and let it lie on the bottom), worms, maggots, bread crust cut into cubes, wheat boiled or plain, pearl barley boiled until it is soft, elderberries, hempseed, and silkweed. This weed, that grows on old woodwork that is long under water (such as lock gates and weir posts), is a great favourite of roach for it harbours minute insects.

PERCH and small boys have a good deal in common. Both species go around in gangs of anything from two to two dozen or more. Both species are rather greedy, rather ferocious, and rather beautiful. In fact, I would say that the perch is more beautiful than the boy, though not nearly so interesting.

Perch are very nearly my favourite fish. The first thing I ever caught was a perch, and anyway perch are wonderfully handsome, with their green-gold bodies barred with black stripes, flaming red fins, huge erect spiky back fins on which it is so easy to prick your finger. Buccaneers of the deep, they are; bold buccaneers with a touch of the gipsy in them.

Since I caught perch when I was a tot, you can take it for granted that perch are easy to catch. Small perch, that is. Big perch are not really difficult to catch, but very few are caught, all the same, and for a good reason: there are few to catch. The perch population is declining: there seem to be many fewer perch in English streams than when I was a boy, about thirty years ago. I suppose the truth is that they are too easy to catch. Greed is their downfall. It seems an awful pity.

Hooking a perch is no trouble *if you can find the perch*. Some ponds and lakes are simply crammed with perch—vast numbers, and none of them more than about four or five inches long. There are so many that the available food supply is not nearly enough for them all to grow big. In such a water you just cannot fail to catch fish, for what they are worth—just toss in almost any old bait, from bacon rind to bootlaces, very nearly, but particularly a lively red worm, and you will have a perch on your hook and several others swimming round him trying to snatch the morsel from his mouth. Oh yes. Two perch at a time are fairly often caught on a spinning lure armed with two hooks.

Such overcrowding is not very common, of course. Some lakes and ponds hold just a few perch or none at all, and you will never find a stream that is overcrowded with perch. In most English rivers the perch are heavily outnumbered by the roach.

But when you *do* hook a perch, whether in river, pond, lake, or canal, be ready for some fun. For since perch always swim around in shoals, catching one means that there are others in the same area, and in a feeding mood, waiting to be caught.

Now here's a word of warning. If you let a perch get away after having hooked him, you can say good-bye to the fishing in that spot. You might just as well move away. For once a perch has escaped after feeling the hook, he seems to tell his friends in the shoal, and off they go, in a body. So you must make certain of landing your perch.

Not that this is particularly difficult, unless he happens to be an extraordinarily large one. Perch are strong and they can fight, but they are usually hooked fairly securely. This is because they are rather ferocious, bullying fish. Unlike, say, the roach, which is rather finicky and cannot always pluck up the courage to mouth the bait, the perch makes a real dash for any attractive morsel that happens to take its fancy. Naturally, such a gobbler gets the bait well inside his big mouth before he realizes that there is something funny about it. It's too late then to think 'Why didn't I keep my big mouth shut?'

On the other hand, a perch's mouth, though big, is rather soft. Fishes' mouths vary enormously, not only in size but in hardness. The pike's, for example, is as hard as bone—in fact, it *is* largely bone. It is quite difficult to drive a hook home into that flinty jaw, but once home, it stays put. Roach have tender mouths, like dace and grayling, and the hook may easily pull out of the soft rubbery tissue. (It isn't *flesh* as we humans know flesh, but rather a mass of cartilage. Some scientists think it quite likely that fish do not feel pain as we do; their nervous system is rather differently arranged. But, of course, they strongly resent the loss of their freedom of movement.) Chub have tough, leathery mouths. Perch come somewhere in between chub and roach. So a perch hooked lightly on the outside of the mouth would be a hard one to hold. That is why you wait before striking a perch until the float has really gone right under. It will bob-o-bob for a time, as the perch sucks the bait in and then blows it out and then sucks it in again. Give him plenty of time, all the time in the world. When he makes up his mind and really closes his mouth on the bait, the float will go under in no uncertain manner. Strike then, and you will be in no real fear of the hook tearing away.

This is all very well, but you haven't hooked one yet. Well, as I say, it's simplicity itself to hook a perch if the perch is there to be hooked. In still water he may be looked for anywhere at all—cruising in mid water, cruising just below the surface, or grubbing along on the bottom. You can lay a lobworm on the bottom and fish for him the dull way, with a ledger, if you like. But perch, being hunters themselves, like a moving bait, and you will perhaps do better if you raise your bait a little off the bottom—and go on raising it, if sport is quiet, until you are fishing only a foot or so below the surface. Don't be afraid to pull your worm about, gently, in the water.

But sport with perch is a bit chancy and unpredictable in still water, unless you are spinning, which is by far the sportiest way of hunting perch. The river is the likelier proposition. In a river, perch might be found almost anywhere except facing the main strength of the current, but in particular they like slow, deep, quiet eddies, where the surface current circles lazily round and round. All the food in that stretch of river comes to the eddy sooner or later—well, most of it, anyway—and fat old perch like to hang around at their ease, out of the mainstream, waiting for the next course to be served up. You must serve them an extra-special course, lowering your baited hook with silent cunning into the slack water, keeping a taut line and waiting for that trembling tug. Give line the moment you feel a fish, and let the perch himself do the rest. A paternoster is the splendid method of hunting perch: you can really search the stream with one, lowering it subtly into spot after spot as you crawl quietly along the bank, with one eye always open for perchy water.

Other perchy water, by tradition, is deep water alongside anything solid, vertical, and man-made. A lock is a wonderful place for a perch, especially if it be disused or used but rarely. Wherever there is timberwork—watch out for timbers that have been sunk to prop up the bank—or even stonework, or of course, brickwork—that is where to hunt perch if the water be fairly deep, as it usually is in such places. But, of course, perch can be found in entirely natural surroundings where there are no man-made structures for them to loll against. (Watch out, by the way, if you hook a perch near an old pile sunk into the bed of the stream. He will know all about the underwater geography of the place, and will teach you a painful lesson in it with pleasure. More than one perch have I known to whip round an old post like a streak of lightning. A broken cast is the inevitable result.)

I'm afraid there is no better bait for a perch, if you are float-fishing, than a worm. The perch I catch nowadays are all caught by spinning a preserved dead minnow or an artificial spinning lure, but the float-fisher had better stick to worms. Maggots will sometimes attract perch, but the vegetarian baits won't, except on very rare occasions.

The RUDD is very like the roach, at a quick glance. In fact, in Ireland it is called the roach. But it is a better fish than any roach that ever swam. Deeper, thicker, more burly and broad-shouldered; handsomer, with its rather golden gleam, its bright red fins and twinkling reddish eye; more sporting and dashing, with its bold habit of feeding right on the surface.

There is another way of telling the rudd from the roach. The back fin of the rudd (called the dorsal fin) is set farther back and the lower lip of the rudd protrudes. (As you might almost expect, the roach has a receding chin. It is in keeping with his character.)

I have to include rudd in this chapter, for they *are* found in running water as well as still. But to be honest, I have never happened to find them in a river. They do not haunt the faster sort of river, but only very placidly flowing streams. It is in lakes that you will find them oftener than not.

I like the rudd. Prime in his favour is the fact that he will take an artificial fly freely (see Chapter 21). But if you have only ordinary float tackle, you can have great sport with him. He has the delightful habit of feeding at or near the surface—and near the bank. You will often see a small clump of reeds quivering as rudd suck off them the insects that cling to them. Try here with a hook on light tackle, unweighted, that sinks slowly. Don't be afraid to fish on the surface with a bit of bread crust and no float at all, just as the fly-fisher fishes his fly. Give your bait a little twitch now and again if there is no immediate response. But if the rudd are there, the chances are that there *will* be an immediate response.

True, the best way of approaching lake rudd is to be out in a boat which is drifted up towards the reeds. But failing that, you can manage quite well if you creep silently round the margin of the lake, casting out over the reeds.

Though particularly partial to small red worms and bread, rudd may be taken on any of the standard roach baits. In fact, river rudd are fished for exactly the same as roach.

The BREAM is a very rum fish. I must confess that I have no great affection for this lumbering lump of almost inanimate matter. But keen bream fishers sometimes catch hundredweights of fish. The only virtue of the bream, as far as I can judge, is his size. The common bronze bream runs large—the record stands at over 13 lb.—and, of course, it is always rather thrilling to feel a fish of several pounds weight on your line. (The silver bream or 'flattie' does not run anything like so large. The record is only $4\frac{1}{2}$ lb., and if you run into a shoal of silver bream you are not likely to get one over a pound and a half, and you will probably catch dozens of useless, slimy little things weighing about two or three ounces apiece.)

The bream is a fish that stands on its head to feed. He has to, for he is immensely deep in the body, though not very far through from side to side. He stands on his head and grubs like a pig on the bottom. When hooked, he is approximately lifeless: size for size, the most faint-hearted fish that swims. A bream of several pounds in weight will come lumbering sheepishly to the net—even on quite fine gut. Not that you need specially fine gut to catch them: they are not particularly intelligent fish. People *do* make a speciality of catching bream, but I do not altogether understand why: I suppose it is the great average weight that attracts folk who like their fish to be big even if otherwise useless.

If you really want to fish seriously for bream, the best thing you can do is to bait up a spot for them, heavily and preferably regularly for several days in advance. Bream are travelling fish; they move slowly around the bed of the lake in shoals, and if you can attract them to one spot and keep them there you will find a lot of fish waiting to be hooked. If you do not have the chance to do a thorough ground-baiting job in advance, watch out for bubbles rising to the surface. These *can* be misleading: they may be nothing more than the sign of gases rising from the bed of the lake to the surface. On the other hand, if you suddenly see a train of bubbles where there have been none before you may reasonably conclude that a shoal of grubbing bream are heading your way. Anyway, toss in a good deal of ground-bait, and fish your baited hook right on the bottom. Very fine tackle is not so urgently necessary. Worms, bread-paste, or maggots will do for bait.

The bite is peculiar to bream—after some preliminary jiggling about, the float may rise in the water and lie flat. This is caused by the bream picking up the bait. Wait until the float slides obliquely under water, and a firm strike makes you a present of a bream. I wish I could work up more enthusiasm for these dull, chicken-hearted, and incredibly slimy fish, but I just can't. (Some people eat bream with relish.)

I can work up a good deal more enthusiasm for EELS. Eels are a nightmare to many fine anglers. They take baits intended for other fish, they can snarl up a cast and line into a terrible tangle, they are horrid to handle, and some people find their snake-like appearance revolting. But there is no getting away from the fact that the eel is a powerful, bold-biting, hard-fighting fish—*if* you can bring yourself to regard it as a fish at all, and not as some odious sort of reptile. (Of course, it *is* a fish.) It is not nice to know, but in the opinion of very many it makes almost the best eating of all fish. I like it myself.

There is no need to tell you how to fish for eels. If you are fishing on the bottom with worms or maggots, and there are eels about, you will find yourself hooking them, whether you want to or not. It is easier to tell you how *not* to catch eels. That is simple; don't use worms or maggots. Eels don't very often take bread, or the other vegetarian baits. Sometimes they will, but not often.

I expect that if you have been fishing at all, you have seen the horrible mess an eel can make of a line, wriggling like a mad thing, in the air and on the grass. This is unnecessary. Never net an eel, never lift it into the air, never put it down on grass. Draw it to the water's edge, draw it gently ashore and put your foot on it. Bend down and cut its head off; or stick your knife in, hard, just behind the head. Your troubles are then over. (All anglers should carry a knife—not just to decapitate eels, but for dozens of reasons.) If there is stonework or brickwork near, or if you happen to have a sheet of newspaper to spread out, an eel will lie on such a surface quietly, and you can unhook it in the ordinary way.

14. Still-water Fish

LET ME ADMIT right away that carp and tench *are* found in rivers—sometimes. But for all practical purposes, unless you happen to live right by one of the few slow-moving rivers in which they are caught in any number, you can forget it and regard them as still-water fish. By far the greater number of carp and tench are caught in ponds and lakes. If you catch them in a river, well, that is practically an accident which happens while you are fishing for something else. I mention this just to keep the record straight. There is no way of making sure that you will 'get among' carp and tench in a river. If you want to fish for them seriously, you must go to still water.

And you must go at the right time of year. Carp and tench are essentially summer fish. June, July, and August are the great months for them. A warm summer will keep them feeding right on through September, but generally speaking the sport begins to go off after the first fortnight of that enchanting month. Sometimes a mild spell right in the middle of winter will wake them up and bring them on the feed—and that will be a red-letter day for you if you happen to be at the right spot at the right time. But generally speaking carp and tench feed heartily during the hot summer months and spend the cold months in a torpor, dug into the mud that covers the bottom of the lakes and ponds which they like best.

Carp fishers are divided into two classes and two only: easy-going casual carp fishers who have never hooked a big one, and passionate addicts who have. For believe me, once you have had a good carp 'on' you will never forget it. Nothing in all angling is quite exactly like the thrill of hooking a big carp.

Notice I say 'hooking.' It is hard enough to hook a big carp, but it is harder still to land it. The man who lands a big carp is an angler.

He is also a man lost to this world. Your serious carp fisher has a strange look in his eye. He is quiet and harmless, but none the less a fanatic. He has tasted an experience which has thrilled him to the core, and as long as he lives he will be wanting to repeat it. He lives and dreams big carp. And big carp demand such single-minded concentration; they ask and deserve a strength of purpose equal to their own. I should say—and I think that all experts will agree with me, for a change—that catching very big carp is the most difficult and uncertain job in all angling. I would also say that catching *any* carp is intensely exciting.

I never fished for carp at all until I was grown up. Then for years I only fished for carp rather casually, just to make a change from other sorts of fishing. I had not caught the 'bug'—or to be more precise, the bug had not bitten me. It follows that I was not very successful. All the same, I managed to catch fish. *Young* carp are quite easy to catch. And I realized that all I had heard about the fighting power of carp was true. A tiddler among carp—say, a two-pounder—fights much harder than, say, a 2-lb. trout. There is no doubt at all that the carp is one of the most powerful, most dogged, and most sporting of all fish. Small or large, wise or reckless, all carp have great fighting hearts. It is fruitless to argue about it, for there can be no certainty; but I have heard it said by very experienced anglers that a carp fights harder, weight for weight, than the kingly salmon. I should say that the carp, the barbel, and the sea trout (not necessarily in that or any order) are the three greatest fighters in our British inland waters. (I would put trout next, and perch after trout, and pike after perch; all very close together. But, of course, you must remember that the fighting power of a fish depends on its condition at the time, and also, to a high degree, on the tackle with which you are fishing.)

Not only is the carp heavy, powerful, and indomitable, but he is intelligent. For a fish, that is. Fish are not as a rule classy thinkers, though their intense timidity sometimes has the same result as intelligence and indeed looks rather like it. But carp, as any experienced fisher will tell you, really do seem to think. They are as timid as any other fish, but they have this extra endowment of cunning, or what looks for all the world like cunning.

For all these reasons, and one or two others which we shall come to shortly, the carp is a thoroughly worthy opponent for any fisher. A good carp catcher must have sound nerves, immense patience, stamina, a quiet mind, and a good conscience. He must also use his brains.

Have I already impressed upon you the fact that a fisherman must go quietly? Forget it. Start all over again. A fisherman who pursues carp must go silently, invisibly, impalpably. He must be as obtrusive as oxygen, as heavy-footed as helium. As noisy as nightfall, as careless as a court of law. You get the idea that a carp fisher is a prudent fellow? Compared with him, rainfall is rowdy.

All this is absolutely necessary because the carp has the eerie faculty of knowing (for instance) the difference between a fishing-rod and the branch of a tree. The carp is not merely cautious; he is something rather different from cautious. He notices anything out of the ordinary as fast as any fish, but whereas a common fish will simply get away from whatever has upset him the carp will stick around (out of range) and think it out. I literally mean that a carp can tell the difference between a rod sticking out over the water and the branch of a tree. Of course, he can't tell the difference between a split-cane rod and a greenheart; he isn't saying to himself: 'That rod wants a coat of varnish.' But he *is* noticing that there is something casting a shadow on the water that was not casting a shadow last time he swam that way. He's as careful as that. And he is quite capable of reasoning to himself that a new shadow is dangerous and on the whole it might be best if he mouthed no bait in that part of the world.

Now then, if a carp is as fastidious as all that about noise and shadows and vibrations, you can imagine that he is pretty fastidious about his food. I'll say he is. The carp is so finicky an eater that it is a standing wonder to me that he grows as big as he does.

It isn't that a carp very much minds *what* he eats. He can be caught on worms, bread (white or brown), bread-paste, bread-paste mixed with honey, bread-paste mixed with chopped onions, gentles, small part-boiled potatoes, and a number of other baits; though those that I have mentioned are undoubtedly the best, and bread or bread-paste is perhaps the best of all. No. What vexes the fisherman and tries his patience almost beyond endurance—*quite* beyond endurance, I'm afraid, in a number of cases—is the carp's fearful finickiness in mouthing a bait that happens to contain a hook.

Take it from me: if the carp has any reason to suspect that there is a hook in the bait or a line attached to it, he will NOT swallow that bait. You have to deceive him absolutely into believing that there are no strings attached to it. And what does that imply?

Why, it means that you must have no float, no weight on the line, no knots even, if you can possibly avoid them. The hook must be completely embedded and concealed in the bait. There must be any amount of slack line so that when the carp picks up the bait he shall not feel the pull of the line. Nor must he even feel the slight vibration which your hand would impart to the rod. You must steal up silently into position, throw out your baited hook, put your rod to rest between *two* forked sticks (see Figure 6), pull a fair amount of line off your reel, and settle down to wait, wait, wait.

That is almost all there is to carp fishing—and oh, what a lot it is! For consider: here is an outline of what a carp fishing session means.

First, you find your water. This—heaven be praised!—is the easiest part of it. It is almost too good to be true, but it *is* true,

Fig. 6

Fig. 6

that almost everywhere in England there are pools and ponds and little lakes and big lakes full of carp. Wales is pretty well provided, too. By and large, wherever you live in England or Wales you will be able to find good carp water. You have only to nose around, and don't be afraid to *ask*. As often as not, carp are to be found in mere bits of ponds, insignificant-looking puddles that no one ever bothers to fish. Never despise them. Ask every farmer you meet if he has a carp pool on his land. You'll be surprised how many have.

Then you make your silent way to the waterside and set up your tackle. Throw in ground-bait if you have it—ground-baiting pays handsomely with carp—and include in it a number of balls of bread-paste just the same size that you will use on your hook. Of course, if you can bait up your pitch regularly for a few days—or nights—before starting to fish it, so much the better. So *very* much the better.

You need a free-running centre-pin reel, or a fixed-spool reel, with a good long line, 100 to 200 yards, of nylon or silk. Your hook, a size 4, 5, or 6, should be tied or whipped direct to the line. (The 'Lenwade' knot shown in Chapter 23 is good for carp fishing.) No float, no shot, no weight of any kind.

Now although carp sometimes cruise in mid water, they are almost invariably caught either right on the bottom or right on the surface. (You can often see and hear them sucking around lily pads, especially when it's hot.)

If you are going to try to catch them on the surface, naturally you won't use ground-bait, which will collect them on the bottom. The trouble is to get your bait (in this case always bread—a big lump of flake) far enough out from the shore. Remember you have no weight to help your casting. A fixed-spool reel (see Chapter 22), is an easy answer, or an 'Adaptacast' platform which turns a centre-pin reel into a fixed-spool reel, and only costs a few shillings.

But if you lack either of these refinements in tackle, you might like to follow my own private tip. This is to drill a clear hole through the centre of an ordinary cork and thread it on to the line. You need a very small shot nipped on to the line, about four feet from the hook, to stop the cork sliding down to the bait. Wrap lead wire round the cork, and you have the weight needed to make a long cast. The big cork will remain awash in the water, if you don't overdo the lead wire. But it will not put any check on the bait when a cruising carp mouths it. If the carp moves away with your sodden bread in his mouth, the line will pass easily through the hole in the cork (which may be lined with a thin copper tube, if you like). The only weight for the carp to take note of is one tiny split shot. Even this can be avoided if you care to go to the trouble of whipping a bristle on the line instead of nipping on the shot. You have to have *something* to stop the cork sliding down to the bait and giving the show away. A blob of sealing-wax will do the trick: but don't blame me if you burn your line.

This way, you see, there is weight for casting, without cumbering up the tackle with *dead* weight on the hook portion of the line. Be sure a carp will notice any dead weight on the line. He will mouth the bait for a long time before he decides to move away with it, and you must make sure that when he decides to move, move he can, with nothing to arouse his suspicions.

ay—if your bread gets sodden and begins to sink, as
n't start hauling in immediately. Give it another half
merged. Anything might happen. And when you feel
you ust wind in to renew your bait—do it slowly.

But the commonest way of angling for carp is with the bait
right on the bottom. Just make sure that your bait has sunk
where your ground-bait sank, pull off a few feet of line from
your reel and make sure that it will not get caught up with twigs
and so on. And wait. Wait. Sit it out. When you see the line
begin to quiver and move out through the rod rings, *go on
waiting*. Don't touch your rod until—after any number of false
alarms—the line really starts to travel out through the rings.
Then seize the rod and in one smooth gesture be on your feet,
pulling it back, with a finger on the reel.

If you have timed it right, neither too fast nor too slow,
neither too early nor too late, you are in for the thrill of your life.
The moment the carp feels that hook go home, he will be off in a
run right across the water that will seem irresistible. Some carp
go fast, some slowly: *all* feel as strong as horses. Keep your rod
point well up and a finger on your reel, and settle down to the
battle of your life.

I've never yet caught a carp over 10 lb., though I'm creeping
up to it. But take my word for it that a 6-lb. carp will tire *you*.
(I forgot to say that your line should be of a breaking strain of
not less than about 7 lb. and not more than about 12 lb.; if you
expect monsters, 15 lb. at the outside. A finer line will be useless.
A much heavier one will have so much dead weight in the water
that it will possibly warn off a sensitive carp.) It's no good trying
to rush even a quite small carp to the net. A battle with even a
moderate young carp—say, about 7 lb.—will take something
like fifteen minutes and upwards.

What makes these combats so intensely thrilling is the
tremendous contrast between the silence and immobility of the
waiting period (which may last for months!) and the ferocity

of the battle once it is joined. And the excitement is much enhanced by the fact that almost all fine carp fishing is had when the light is off the water. Night time is the classic time for carping. When dusk falls, bats fly, and rats rustle, you can begin to expect action. You can fish all night in the expectation of huge excitements, and I should say that the most hopeful moment of all is just before dawn. And since the best of all carp waters are tree-fringed, silent, remote, and brooding lakes, you can imagine that there is something rather eerie, even chilling, in this rare and solemn sport. But carp *are* sometimes caught by day, so don't despair if the thrill of dusk and night fishing is denied you. But do try, one day, to get to the waterside by dawn.

Two last words on carp. Big baits catch big fish. (This is true of almost all fish, but especially, perhaps, of carp.) And—use a strong rod. A pike rod will do.

TENCH I know less about. They are fine, handsome fish, dark olive-green, deep in the body, compact, muscular, with fine glowing red eyes. You fish for them on the bottom, preferably with smallish red worms. They share a number of characteristics with carp, though they do not grow nearly so large. (The record tench stands at $7\frac{1}{2}$ lb.; the record carp at 44 lb.) But a pounder is a nice fish. Naturally, you angle for them with finer tackle than you dare use for carp. You use a slender float, and fish right on the bottom; and you may find that the float trembles for a longish time before it slides under. Dawn is the best time for tench fishing. A two-pounder will make you wish you had tied the knots in your tackle with a bit more care. I never fish for tench myself, preferring to go flat-out for carp whenever I do any still-water fishing. But if you hear of any tench fishing in your locality, go to it. It is good fun. Unfortunately there is nothing to do with a tench except put him back again. I never actually heard of anyone eating tench; whereas carp are delicious if you have someone at home prepared to go to endless trouble in the cooking of them.

15. River Fish

I DID ONCE catch a gudgeon in a lake, and either a dace or a chub, I forget which. But that was rather unusual: someone may have caught them in a river and put them there. Normally, all these fish are river fish, and so are the barbel, ruffe, and bleak.

The barbel you would have to fish for specially, deliberately; meaning to catch one and going out of your way to do it. All the others you might catch without malice aforethought: they figure in a mixed bag such as any general fisher who merely sets out for a day's sport may find in his keep-net at the end of the day.

The CHUB we have mentioned before, when we were talking about long-trotting. Yes, that is the most reliable way of catching chub, I think. The point about the chub is that he doesn't seem much put out by the sight of your tackle, but he will be very much upset by the sight of *you*. You must tread lightly, for he is a demon for picking up the vibrations of a footfall—and just to make it more difficult, he is a fish who likes loitering near the bank, preferably under overhanging trees. So by far the most sensible method of float fishing for chub is to drift a bait down to him on a long line.

He is a grabber, the chub. He pouches the bait and down goes the float, under in one. There is no hesitation about a chub bite, and he is a fairly easy fish to hook. But his first rush, when he feels the hook, is something to watch out for. Since the chub favours 'bank lies' (what a nice phrase!) he is never far away from underwater obstructions such as the interlacing roots of trees—and if he gets your cast tied round a root in his first dash, well, that is one knot that you will never unravel. But if you can hold him hard enough to bring him up out of his lair in the first few moments of the battle, he will soon give in. He is a sprinter, the chub, with not much stamina to back up his first wild lunge.

Fortunately, he is a greedy chap and will eat practically anything. The standard chub baits are legion—it is shorter to tell you what he will *not* eat. He will not eat bread-paste mixed with curry powder. I know, because I tried. But anything else that you can think of—all the bread-paste mixtures, bread cubes, cubes of banana, worms, maggots, cherries, currants, strawberries, small fish, bacon, bits of meat, snails, frogs, flies. There is no limit, it seems, to the adventurousness of the chub—viewed as a gourmet, that is. It is about the only way in which he *is* adventurous, I'm afraid.

As you will see in Chapters 19 and 21, chub can be caught very happily by spinning and by fly-fishing; but the float fisher can get them too.

The DACE is a delightful little fish. Unfortunately the emphasis is rather on that word 'little.' If only the dace grew to a noble size, what a noble fighter he would be! Ounce for ounce, he will fight as hard as anything that swims, I think: but one tends to leave the dace right out of the strength-for-weight computations, because ordinarily 4 oz. is a moderately fair weight for a dace, and you really can't begin to talk of a four-ouncer in the same breath as a four-pounder. Still, a mighty fine little fish he is, as game, as bold, as tenacious, as intrepid, as beautiful as any trout. Oh, if only he grew big! (Dace *are* caught about a pound in weight, every season, but they are the exceptions. That is to say, on most waters they would be exceptions. Just one or two marvellous rivers, such as the Hampshire Avon and the Berkshire Kennet, breed big dace, with several pounders coming to net every year. The record stands at $1\frac{1}{2}$ lb. and a four-ouncer, as I said before, is a moderate fish.)

You see I have plenty of prejudices—or, rather, of personal preferences—about fishes. I suppose they have no place, really, in what sets out to be a practical and plain textbook. But there it is: if you have any strong feeling for fish at all, you have strong preferences for certain fish as fish. At least, *I* have. You have gathered that I think very little of the bream, that dullard, and not so very much of the roach, old sheepie. Well, I don't mind admitting that I take a very personal view of fish: I like them or dislike them or am indifferent to them. My fishing is never cold and calculating and impersonal: there is always an element of *feeling* in it which makes it (I find) even more interesting. I fish very well for fish which I happen to like, very badly for fish for which I have no feelings at all. Fish that I actively *dislike* I pursue with an almost vindictive ferocity, a true hunter's determination. In truth, the only fish for which I feel real antagonism is the brutal old pike. Perhaps he is not so bad as I paint him—trout are just as savage, really—but he is bully enough to make me quite enjoy hunting him. Well, it may be foolish, but that's how I feel about fish. And the dace is a fish for which I have any amount of admiration.

In addition to his other virtues, the dace feeds at the surface. I quite agree that there is a great, mysterious fascination in hooking unseen fish deep down in the secret depths; certainly there is; but there is also great joy in seeing your fish and picking him out, individually, on the surface. The dace takes a fly well, but here we are considering him as a bait-taker. He is not so omnivorous as the chub, but prefers such dainty morsels as a scrap of bread crust, a tiny pellet of paste on a 16 hook, a single maggot, or a small red worm. Dace also hit freely at hempseed, elderberry, wheat, currants, and pearl barley.

Dace hit freely, say I: but you, the fisher, must hit freely, too, if you are to hook a dace. The dace's bite is the fastest you will ever have to handle. You can always tell it—a lightning dip of the float, no preliminary fooling around, just that quick dip. Almost always, the float moves slightly sideways as well as down. In a sense, it is an easier bite than the roach's, for the roach is almost too careful to live, and his bite makes itself manifest (though not *very* manifest) in so many different ways. But the dace's bite is that unvarying bold dip of the float. You always see it—but you are a smart man if you twist your wrist in time to hook the flash of lightning at the other end. Say you hook one bite in four: that is plenty good enough to be going on with. I wish I could.

Dace are not very shy fish, really. They will stand a fair amount of inspection at close quarters. *Big* dace are only caught, as far as I can discover, by a sort of moderately long long-trotting, with the bait well down. But ordinary, average dace are as often as not hooked on a short line with the bait a foot or so—or even a few inches—below the surface. Frail tackle is obviously an advantage in a way—it handles very delicately (except in a high wind!) and enables you to use a tiny float which suits the quarry better. There is something almost indecent about fishing for so small and quicksilvery a fish with hefty tackle better suited to chub or carp.

Dace swim in shoals, and you can locate them by eye. In summer, they play near the surface, taking midges and invisibly small smuts from the surface, playing and gambolling with the winning light-heartedness of lambs. If you cast your tiny bait among them, it is very likely indeed that a dace will be at it before your float has cocked. It is real fast work, dace fishing, and the most delightful fun. In winter, you swim a bait down deeper, near the bottom, just as you would for roach. Ground-baiting is a help, I suppose—cloud, or a few maggots tossed into the head of the swim now and again. There is no ground-bait for dace more influential than hempseed. They love it, and many a time I have used it as a ground-bait while hooking fish with a split shot nipped on to the bend, or a fragment of bicycle valve rubber slipped well clear of the barb, of a white-painted hook.

Some people confuse young chub with mature dace, or vice versa. Apart from the fact that the dace is more silvery, and rather more shapely, there is one certain identification. The anal fin—that is the fin underneath, at the rear—is convex in the chub, concave in the dace. You soon learn, too, to distinguish the chub's great big mouth with white, rubbery lips. The dace has a neat little mouth—one reason why you must use a neat little bait on a neat little hook.

The BARBEL is so great a fish that anglers always speak of him with awe. You can class him with the carp as the Superfish of the 'coarse fish' category. I think he is not so cunning as the carp, but there is no denying that he shares the carp's mysterious remoteness from the ordinary, everyday traffic of the float. Just as the carp is fished for by single-minded specialists who think of nothing else, so is the barbel. There are two big differences between them, though: barbel live in the strongest running water, whereas carp haunt the silent pools; and barbel are uneatable, whereas carp, properly prepared, are sumptuous food.

For some obscure reason, I cannot bring myself to spend a great deal of time angling for fish which are uneatable, even by the cat. That is why, though I have had great sport with chub, I no longer count myself a serious chub fisher. And a barbel fisher I shall never become. A pity this would be, perhaps, were there not noble alternatives to the barbel—for he grows to an immense size. The record stands at 14 lb. 6 oz., and there is no doubt in the minds of serious barbel fishers that fish of 20 lb. haunt the Thames and the Hampshire Avon, to name two champion barbel waters. (Another good one is the Trent.) And for desperate, rod-smashing fury of the fight, the barbel is hard indeed to beat. The only one I ever caught was a child of 3 lb. odd—and that took so much landing that I dread to think what would happen if I hit one of a dozen pounds. Like tigers they fight; their hard lives, lived in the constant strain of racing water, make them muscular in the extreme and breed stamina into their hearts. It is a pity, I can't help feeling, that when you have lived through the throbbing excitement of such a fight, all you have on your hands is a distinctly ugly, lank-looking, drab-coloured fish with a distinct sneer on his face and four barbules hanging from his lips. There is nothing to do with him but put him back. That is why I only once fished for barbel. But, of course, you don't have to share my curious views on these matters.

I must in duty bound tell you how barbel are caught. I know, for some of my friends are fine barbel men, even if I am not one myself. The barbel is a summer fish, generally speaking. Unlike almost any other fish, he haunts the powerful water, glorying in his strength to defy any current, until autumn closes down on the world like woodsmoke from a fire. Then the barbel silently disappears, slipping unnoticed away from the lashing weir stream and the racing glide, proud and scornful, taking up his winter quarters in deep, deep holes wherein he broods through the long winter, unseen and (in the main) uncaught.

Take stout tackle with you to the weir stream, or search him out in fast, shallow runs over gravel. He eats worms for prefer-ence, maggots if you have no worms. Ledger for him, with a big worm and a hook-length not finer than 2X, or send your float sliding down the stream with a bunch of maggots or a worm dragging right on the bottom—he *always* feeds on the bottom, never raising his snout from the gravel he loves. Ground-baiting for barbel used to be a ritual, no less, with literally thousands and thousands of lob worms being unloaded into the swim days beforehand. We can't afford the worms, now that they cost up to a penny each. And, I gather, just as many barbel are caught now as used to be caught in the 'good old days.' You can toss in, if you like, balls of clay containing worms—it has to be something pretty solid, to stand up to the speed and strength of barbel water. But it seems to me that if it is a barbel swim, it is a barbel swim, and the barbel are there already. So don't despair if you haven't worms to spare.

In any gently flowing stream you are as likely as not to see hordes of flashing little silver fish, none more than two or three inches in length, milling around at the surface. No, not dace: these imps are BLEAK. They are useful as dead bait to the spinner, who mounts them on a spinning flight (see Chapter 19). I don't know what other use they are. They can be a confounded nuisance if you are fishing for something bigger, for they will mob your bait as soon as it hits the water. If you want to catch them, a fragment of paste on a small hook, fished a few inches below your float, will do the trick. Your float tip must only show a fraction of an inch above the water, for if it shows more it will be more than the bleak can do to pull it under, and instead of striking you will be wasting your time and wearing out your nerves watching a float going blobbety-bob. If you want to get rid of a shoal of bleak, toss a piece of bread on to the water. They will happily mob it, drifting downstream out of your way like a crowd of ladies at a bargain sale.

RUFFE (or POPE) are a small fish much despised, even hated, by many sound anglers. They lurk at the bottom, generally not far from the main current, and just where you would expect to find something bigger and better. They will bite your worm boldly, making you think that you have a real fish—then up comes a miserable little thing not four inches long, looking rather like a perch from which all the glorious colour has faded. The same sharp-spined dorsal fin, the same big mouth—and an extra, nasty little spine on the gill plate which will prick you if you are not careful over the unhooking. All reasons to abominate the ruffe, yes: *but*—ruffe happen to be nice eating. Just for that reason and no other, it is sometimes worth while actually to fish for ruffe, if you have nothing better on your mind. A little red worm will fetch them, and you needn't be particular about the size of hook.

Finally, the GUDGEON. Now this is another little fish that deserves better of anglers than he gets. True, he stays small—a two-ounce gudgeon is good, and three ounces is enormous—

but he has a number of virtues. First, he will go on biting on the hottest day, when everything in the river seems to have called it a day and gone to sleep. (Chub, too, I should confess, are bonny feeders on a hot day, but you need a fly rod, really, to do much good with them then.) Secondly, the gudgeon is the most undemanding of fish—he will go on biting even when you are standing in the river with your feet in the middle of a shoal of him. Thirdly, he is delicious eating. This used to be very well known, and 'gudgeon parties' of ladies and gentlemen used to take a punt on the Thames just for the purpose of catching great quantities of the little fish for 'a fry of gudgeon.' (That shows you how obliging he is: I can't imagine any other fish being caught by a punt-load of ladies and gentlemen. But it seems to have been forgotten, and you hear more curses than praise when an angler has happened to get among a mob of these drab-looking little fish. If only they would accept their luck, catch a panful, and try them fried in breadcrumbs, they might change their tune.)

You don't bother to ground-bait for gudgeon: you just stir up the bottom of the water with a stick. (This is a very old trick, not much practised here any more, but still fairly common on the Continent of Europe, where they take their coarse fishing even more seriously than we do here. Because they eat more coarse fish.) The discoloration of the water attracts fish always—you will always be well advised to look for fish near or just downstream of a cattle-drink. It has just exactly the same effect as cloud ground-bait—it brings inquisitive, sharp-eyed fish to look into this suspended matter, which may or may not contain scraps of food.

You will not always find gudgeon, of course, but when you do, you can go on pulling them out until there isn't one left in the shoal. Game, greedy, and stupid to the last, they will grab your scrap of red worm, your single maggot, or your pellet of paste as if they were starving.

And what a thump a gudgeon gives to a float! Down it goes as if a real good fish were biting. I have seen the top of a rod that was supporting a ledger flip downwards as if a barbel had hit the bait—and up came a gudgeon, much to the chagrin of the ledgerer.

There are also minnows, sticklebacks, loach or loaches, and the miller's thumb. You are welcome to the lot. They are truly the 'small fry' of the water, unattractive even to a fisher so modest in his ambitons as me. (Though minnows, of course, are much used as spinning lures—caught, killed, preserved, and mounted on special flights. See Chapter 19.)

I think we have dealt with all the fish you are likely to angle for in Britain, except the trout, the salmon, the grayling, and the pike. Trout and grayling are considered in the chapter on fly-fishing (Chapter 20). Salmon are beyond the scope of this modest book—and this impecunious angler. Pike are a different matter, and we will get after them right now.

PART IV: PIKE

<><><><><><><><><><><><><><><><><><><><><><><><><>

16. The Cannibal King

<><><><><><><><><><><><><><><><><><><><><><><><><>

PIKE. Yes, no doubt about it, that is a name to conjure with.
A surly, dramatic, crisp, challenging monosyllable. Pike. What
a reputation the pike has! Much of it, maybe, unwarranted by
the facts. But enough hard fact can be disentangled from the
wealth of fiction surrounding the pike to know that he deserves a
good proportion of the notoriety which attends his name. The
pike is a bad, bad fish, the fish of legend and story.

In part, the pike's reputation for wickedness springs from his
appearance, which is savage indeed. That long, lean body,
with dorsal and anal fins set far back to assist the great tail in
giving him prodigious acceleration from a standing start. That
subtle camouflage that enables him to lurk unseen in weeds until
little fish swim within reach of his jaws. Those jaws themselves
—huge for the size of his body, bony-hard, armed with innumerable sharp teeth, raked backwards so that a fish may enter but
never leave those grim portals. Yes, the pike looks the part—
the part of the cannibal king, the tiger of the underwater jungle,
the killer of the deeps, the freshwater shark, and any other
uncomplimentary names that have been bestowed on him.

To be utterly fair to the pike, he is not the only one to mis-
behave. Trout of all ages, I am quite convinced, are cannibals
little less greedy than the pike. The perch is no less an eater of
small fish. Chub eat minnows, too. They are all tarred with the
same brush, that quartet of savages.

But the pike gets the worst of it for two reasons. First, he looks the part. Secondly, he grows to such an enormous size. The record British fish may be 47½ lb. (it is not yet confirmed), and a fish of 53 lb. was caught on rod and line in Lough Conn, Eire, by a lucky Mr Garvin who the same day took one of over 30 lb. It is known that pike eat ducklings, moorhens, and rats; and legends (I would put them no higher) tell of pike seizing the lips of horses going to the water to drink. Naturally, there are even stories of pike attacking swimmers, which I do not believe. Anyway, the pike is a big enough handful for any-one. The fact that he only eats smaller fish when he is hungry, and will let them swim around his head at other times, does not alter the fact that a pike in the water means havoc among other fish. Keepers of costly trout waters harry the pike mercilessly, and rightly. But in a nice mixed fishing it is just as well to have some pike in the water, and not only for the pleasure of catching them. A decent head of pike keeps the other fish from multi-plying unduly. There are many instances where lack of pike has allowed the roach to increase so plentifully that there just is not anywhere near enough food to go round, with the result that the average size of the roach is miserably small. But this is by the way. There is just one more thing to be said against the pike, and we have done. He eats *nothing else besides* other fish. That is what sets him apart from his fellow cannibals, the trout, the perch, and the chub. Their cannibalism is occasional, his is permanent.

You can catch pike in ponds, lakes, canals, and rivers—but even in rivers, you will look for them in the queter parts. The pike, for all his ferocity, is no barbel, to brave the current for its own sake. He is an idle, skulking fish, that loves to sidle along the weed-beds, lurking and creeping and hiding until his prey is within a short strike. He is not, curiously enough, a very good swimmer: all his mettle is in his tremendous acceleration. Like the chub, he is a sprinter rather than a stayer.

What do you reason out from all that? Why, that you must take your bait to the pike, not expect the pike to search out your bait. Lazybones will hang around in the weeds until he feels sure of getting a meal with the least exertion. And there is something else you might deduce from a knowledge of the pike's habits—he prefers to take an injured fish rather than a healthy and active one. If it comes to a choice between lancing himself through the water after a lively, active dace, and a crippled, limping roach, there is no doubt which he will prefer. So it obviously will pay you to fish for him (*a*) where he lies, and (*b*) with a bait that deludes him into the belief that he is on to a soft touch.

One way of doing this, you will hardly need to be told, is by live-baiting. I will explain it to you, because I think that if you have paid money for a book on fishing, you are entitled to know the principle basic techniques in current use. But let me say again that I do so reluctantly. I never use live baits nowadays, and I never will. It is a form of fishing which does not appeal to me any more. It means inflicting injury—slight, I agree—on a small fish, and then condemning it to cruise miserably around, perhaps for hours, until it is seized by a pike, or dies. A thoroughly horrid business of which no angler can be proud. I have no pity for the pike—he is intent on grabbing little fish and eating them, and he meets a tiger's end. Nor have I the least compunction about killing fish. They are a lower order of life which man may put to his own uses. But long-drawn-out, lingering misery—that is an abhorrent prospect. I will tell you about live-baiting, because if *I* don't, somebody else will—you only have to walk along the water's edge to see it in operation, wherever pike are fished for. But I most earnestly beg of you never to use this foully unsporting method of catching fish. It is idle, evil, and thoroughly unsporting. Read about it, then turn your face against it, and learn the grand, sporting, thrilling, and delightful practice of spinning, which is a wonderful way of catching pike and other fish. (Chapters 17, 18, and 19.)

Mind you, I must admit that I *have* live-baited for pike. I do not deny it. I used that method before I knew any better.

Here goes. The beastly business consists of catching a small fish—roach, dace, gudgeon, carp, chub, something like that—and sticking a big hook into it. These great hooks are normally two in number, and are 'trebles'—that is to say, three-pronged hooks, which are not very clever hooks anyway. Usually one prong of one hook is stuck into the bait's back, near the dorsal fin, and one prong of the other hook is hooked into its gill-plate. A fat float is fixed on the line, the poor bait is tossed into the water to cruise frantically up and down, trying all the time to get into weeds and hide, until a pike sees it. When the float goes under and stays under you can congratulate yourself on the fact that a pike has seized the bait and is turning it in his mouth (pike generally strike broadside, and then turn the bait so that they swallow it head-first). You then raise your rod tip, give a tremendous, solid strike to pull those big hooks home into that bony jaw, and start to play your fish.

Another method of live-baiting, much used when smaller live-baits are in use (minnows, when out for perch, say), is to pass one large single hook through the lips of the bait, or pass one large single hook through a lump of flesh near the dorsal fin, and proceed as before. People who use this single-hook technique have to wait even longer before they strike, to make sure that the bait is all inside the mouth of the predatory fish. It is often halfway down the gullet, and then you hook the perch or pike right down inside, which is a filthy business.

To finish this grisly business, I must tell you that if you are a live-baiter for pike you will need a rod with a good stout tip—not to fight the pike with, but to stand the deadweight strain as you swing the live-bait over the water—a free-running reel of any kind, and a line of not less than ten or a dozen pounds breaking strain. You will also need some of those ghastly treble hooks on wire, called 'snap-tackles.' Any tackle shop will cheerfully sell you one, it being still legal. I hope that it will not be legal much longer. The old custom of the 'gorge' bait, which involved threading a wire through the body of a living fish and a hook which invariably took hold right down in the pike's stomach, was legal when I was a boy and even when I was a young man. It is illegal now, and there is no earthly reason why all forms of live-baiting should not follow it into the limbo of cruel practices which we have very slowly grown out of. I appeal to you to learn to spin. You will catch just as many pike, with ten times the pleasure and excitement. And you will still be able to think of yourself as a sportsman.

(You *can* use an elastic band to fix the hooks to the live-bait—but it will still suffer all the tortures of terror.)

That is all I want to say about live-baiting. But assuming that you do fish for pike—and I hope fervently that it will be with a spinning lure—you want to know a few things about striking and playing this terror of the placid water. Yes, indeed, playing a pike is great stuff—and, incidentally, a pike fights vastly harder on spinning tackle than on the other. Naturally, for his mouth is not gagged wide open by the corpse.

It is no exaggeration to say that you must hit a pike just as hard as your tackle will stand. The roof of his mouth is hopeless for a hook-hold—it is pure bone and teeth. The secret is to take a *sideways* swipe at him—swing the rod hard one way or the other, instead of raising it vertically. The best hook-hold is the big muscular cartilage alongside the lower jaw.

Once a pike feels you, he will start his first run. It will probably not be a long run—as I said, pike are sprinters—but it will be strong. Try to put a lot of sidestrain on him if he is heading for weeds. It is particularly important to keep a tight line on a pike, because if the line goes slack and he gets a bite at the trace with those teeth, he might easily nip it through.

You will find the pike a dead-sluggish, craven fighter in high summer, but by October he is beginning to firm up, fully recovered from the exertions of spawning in the spring, and getting a fair muscular tone. The winter pike, like the winter roach and the winter chub, is an utterly different proposition from the laggard of summer, the floppy, flabby, and flaccid fighter (save the word!) who gives up after one little rush. Yes, the winter pike will bore deep and pull hard, but you will surely have him out if you keep a solid strain on him and keep his teeth away from that trace. There is just one thing about playing a pike that differs from playing doctrine as it applies to all other fish. When a pike stands on his tail and thrusts his great fierce head up out of the water, shaking it viciously in an effort to rid himself of the hook, then you do *not* drop the rod point (as you would with any other fish that jumped on the surface). Instead, you hang on hard and pray that the hook-hold is good and true. When a trout leaps, for instance, you drop the rod tip smartly, or he will smash the line as he flops down. But if you give a surfacing, head-shaking pike a slack line, he will shake that hook out as sure as fish lay eggs.

(They *do*, in case you didn't know. The female fish lays her many eggs in a shallow depression which she scoops out of the bottom with flicks of her tail, preferably in a calm and shallow place. The male fish drops his fertilizing milt over them, and some fish then cover the eggs with gravel or sand by a flick of the tail. Fish often find the eggs and eat them. Those which do hatch out give birth to tiny fish called fry. Most of these are eaten by other fish. A tiny proportion escape the acute perils of childhood and grow up. All the so-called 'coarse fish'—those which we have been discussing—spawn in spring, which is why we have a rigid close season between 15 March and 15 June, both dates inclusive. Trout, on the other hand, spawn in the autumn, which is why the close season for trout lasts roughly from the end of September to the beginning of April—it varies slightly according to the locality.)

To get back to pike. You will find them always near the weeds. They are solitary fish from infancy, given much to roaming and skulking. The tail-end of a little island is a good place to look for a pike, and so is the junction of a small stream with a large one. Anywhere they can hide and prey on passing little fish is a likely place for a pike. If you see small fish breaking the surface, skittering along the top and leaping clean out into the air, you can safely say that a pike is working among them. Or perhaps it is a perch, but the answer comes to the same thing in terms of your immediate action, which is to put your bait into the water where you saw the disturbance.

Remember that a pike always strikes upwards, so keep your lure near the surface—at least, keep it well off the bottom. A pike, like a perch, will have a go at a tremendous lure, anything up to half its own size or even bigger than that.

Pike seem to feed according to a sort of cycle of hunger and repletion. They will suddenly come on the feed and eat ravenously for about two or perhaps even three days—no one is quite sure how long the feeding bee lasts, and no doubt it much depends on how much food the pike finds and how easily—and then they will go off into a complete coma, and you might as well stay at home. The weather is said to affect pike fishing—it is said to affect all sorts of fishing, for that matter—but I don't know, I wonder. One thing is fairly sure: when we have had a long succession of blazing hot days and the water is low and warm and lacking in oxygen, then all fish are lethargic just as we humans are. That is pretty sure. Apart from that one sad certainty, I have no great faith in all the old saws about the weather and its effect on angling. There is that old jingle:

> *When the wind is in the south,*
> *It blows the bait into the fishes' mouth.*
>
> *When the wind is in the north,*
> *The prudent fisher goes not forth.*
>
> *When the wind is in the west,*
> *Then the fisher loves it best.*

And, of course, there is an almost universally believed legend that an east wind puts a stop to fishing. Well, I have no faith in any of that bag of tricks. I think that what it boils down to is this: if the weather suits *you*, it will probably suit the fish. If the barometer is falling, you don't feel any too perky and neither do the fishes. If the glass is rising, you feel rather more spry than when it is falling, and fishes likewise. With the proviso that fish are very much more sensitive to atmospheric changes than we are, and probably feel the high pressure and the low pressure before our relatively coarse systems do. I have caught fish in every sort of weather including fog (which is said to be fatal), and I certainly do not believe that old saw about hard frost being good for perch and pike fishing. Hard cold puts perch and pike off their feed: they lie around miserably, waiting for it to warm up—just as humans do. If pressed, I would say that the best weather for pike fishing would be the second day of a thaw after a hard, long frost.

PART V: SPINNING

~~~~~~

17. The Big Idea

~~~~~~

I DO NOT know who invented spinning. I wish I did, for I would willingly pray for the repose of his soul. He was a genius, no less.

Someone once noticed that fish of the predatory sort dashed through the water and caught smaller fish who were either taken by surprise or just could not put on a good enough turn of speed. Someone else—and this was the genius—thought how sensible it would be to draw through the water a bit of bone or metal to which he had cunningly attached a hook. This was the birth of spinning. It took place a very long time ago. It is still practised today—by, I am glad to say, ever-increasing numbers of anglers, who are discovering that it is the most exciting method of catching fish bar only fly-fishing. (And some, who are perfectly entitled to their opinions, find it even more exciting than fly-fishing.)

That is the basis of spinning, then—to fix a hook to something that will delude a fish into believing that it is a small fish he sees swimming along. This 'something' can take any of a huge variety of forms, but the basic idea is always the same—to persuade a predatory fish that it is a small fish which he might as well grab. Sometimes it *is* a fish, killed and mounted on a spinning flight which gives it the semblance of life.

The word 'spinning' indicates that the lure spins in the water. Sometimes it does, but just as often it is not a true spinning lure but a lure which wobbles, lurches, flops, and tumbles about in the water. The important thing is that it should give off enough *flash* to attract the attention of the predatory fish. The vibration of the lure is another important part of its attractiveness—often a predatory fish is made aware of a lure which he would not have *seen*, by the vibrations which its passage sets up in the water.

That is all there is to the great idea of spinning. Now let us consider what we need and how we go about it.

18. Tackle and Technique

UNFORTUNATELY, spinning tackle is fairly highly specialized—you can hardly spin with the same rod that you use for your float fishing. You can make some sort of rudimentary shot at it, true, but so sure as you pick up the trick of doing some sort of spinning with your float-fishing rod, so surely will you get the itch to own a true spinning outfit. And why not, indeed? I hope that you will end by owning float, spinning, and fly outfits. Pick them up piece by piece as you go along; it's part of the fun of fishing.

The most important item of a spinner's equipment is his reel. There are many sorts of spinning reel, but there is only one feature that a spinning reel *must* have: all the rest are refinements. A spinning reel must allow the lure, as it is sent sailing through the air, to pull off line freely, without hindrance. Obviously, a reel that turns very easily is the thing for you. There is plenty of choice, but nothing is intrinsically better than the old-fashioned free-running 'Nottingham'-style reel, made of wood or metal. (A wooden reel with a metal lining and a 'star-back' of brass to give it rigidity and prevent it warping is the finest reel anyone could wish for. If you can pick up a sound one second hand you will be on to a good thing. Treasure it.)

Mr Thurlow Craig, that prince of pike-hunters, has told how he lightened an ordinary old Nottingham wooden reel by judicious drilling, and found it one of the most effective spinning-reels. I, too, like spinning with the old wooden reel. In its original state there is rather a lot of inertia to be overcome at the start of the cast—hence the drilling. But if you start drilling a reel, you must be careful not to unbalance it. Perhaps the very best of all the straightforward old-style centre-pin spinning reels is the 'Aerial' made by Messrs Allcocks. This is a light metal reel of perfect workmanship and considerable line capacity. An 'Aerial' will certainly serve you perfectly both for float fishing and for spinning. But an 'Aerial' is in the Rolls-Royce class; it costs money.

A delightful reel to spin with is the 'multiplier' type. The spool or drum of a multiplier is exceedingly light, which accounts for the fact that, having little inertia to overcome, a comparatively light lure will easily pull off a good length of line —a more technical way of saying that you can cast a light lure a long way. But such reels need to be accurately machined, and the cheaper ones are not always perfectly satisfactory in this respect. These reels are called multipliers because of a chain of gears which enable you to retrieve line fast while turning the reel handle slowly—about three and a half turns of the spool to one turn of the handle is probably the average ratio.

Finally there is the fixed-spool reel. This works on a different principle entirely. The spool or drum does not revolve at all (as the name implies). The axis of the spool is at right angles to the axis of the rod, and line falls over the end of the spool in a series of loops. If you hold a cotton reel end-on to your eye and pull off cotton, you will see the principle at work. Since there is absolutely no resistance, apart from a little friction in the line itself, a light lure can be cast an amazing distance with a fixed-spool reel. When it comes to reeling in again, a revolving 'flier' catches the line, and winds it back on to the spool. It is a brilliant idea, but one snag is that, when playing a fish, you are never in direct contact with it as you are with a conventional reel. You are turning the flier round and round the spool, laying on loop after loop of line, but you do not actually feel the strength of the fish. It is rather like fighting a duel with loofahs. These reels are wonderfully effective and I have no desire to decry them, but I like to feel that I am in direct contact with my fish, not playing him through a sponge.

The high cost of a fixed-spool reel and its muzziness and lack of definition when playing a fish are overcome by a remarkably simple, brilliant invention known as the 'Adaptacast.' This is a simple, spring-loaded turntable, costing only a few shillings, which enables you to turn your old-style centre-pin reel at right angles to the rod for casting (giving you, in effect, the cast of a fixed-spool reel), and to turn it back into the normal position the moment your bait hits the water—which puts you in direct touch with the fish, when you hook one. You just reel in as usual. I am fascinated by the simplicity of this little invention.

You can learn all about the use of the fixed-spool reel in Chapter 22. But I am sure that you should first learn to cast with a free-running centre-pin reel. Master that first and all shall be added unto you.

Well, let's learn. Accuracy in aiming the lure will only come (if it comes at all!) with long practice; and so will distance. All I or anyone else can tell you, in print, is the fundamental point that *throughout the flight of the lure your thumb or finger must maintain perfect control of the drum.* I say 'thumb or finger' because if you have the reel mounted under the rod, in the position you are accustomed to with float fishing, then you will find your finger the most convenient instrument to control the drum. If you mount your reel for spinning on top of the rod— *all* multipliers are mounted on top of the rod—then your thumb will fall most readily into the controlling.

But, finger or thumb, it must be ready to brake that drum. You see, when you have reeled up your chosen lure to within a yard or less from the rod tip, swung the rod backwards a little and then hard forwards, releasing the trapped line as the lure begins to pull out—when you have done that, you have set up a fairly powerful force to pull line off the reel. The initial tug sets the free-running drum revolving at some speed—faster, in fact, than the line itself can get out through the rod rings, which inevitably slow it down. Now if the reel goes on revolving faster than the line is running away through the rod rings, the result will be that line wraps itself back round the spool—in the wrong direction. This is what is known, sorrowfully, as a 'bird's-nest'—a frightful tangle of loops and knots that looks as if it will never be unravelled. (It always *can* be unravelled, actually, but you will waste ten minutes or so of fishing time in sorting it out.)

So you brake the drum with your thumb or forefinger as the lure flies out over the water. Gently, of course, just a smooth pressure which keeps the speed of the spool down to a reasonable rate of r.p.m. Only experience—several days of experience—can teach you just how hard, or how lightly, to brake the spool in differing circumstances of lure-weight, line-weight, wind, and power of throw.

As the lure gets well out over the water, the various factors resolve themselves into a simple equation, and you can ease up your finger pressure and let the reel revolve as it will. But as the lure slows down and its parabola through the air begins to decline, you need to brake the reel again—or it will go on revolving, again, faster than line is being taken off, with the same old bird's-nest piling up for your delectation.

That is the simple principle of casting with a centre-pin reel. If you use an 'Adaptacast,' or a fixed-spool reel, casting is child's play, since there is no mechanical possibility of an over-run or a bird's-nest. If you use a multiplier, you adopt a slightly different technique. Whereas with a centre-pin reel the sideways swing is the usual cast, with a multiplier you can use the upright cast. That is to say, bring the rod up until the lure is hanging down just behind your right shoulder and flick it forwards and upwards, aiming high up into the air. Most beginners find the lure falling at their feet the first few times they try to cast with a multiplier and the short rod that usually accompanies it. Lob it up, *up*—and it should sail through the air with a high trajectory. You brake the spool with your thumb just as you braked the centre-pin reel.

So much for types of reel and the essential mechanics of casting. Rods are a problem, too. A spinning-rod should be fairly flexible right down to your hand, but the tip must be stout enough to stand the tremendous strain of throwing lures weighing up to as much as an ounce or more. Perhaps an ounce or two doesn't sound much, when a rod with a tip no thicker than a matchstick can handle a fish weighing several pounds: but there is all the world of difference between playing a fish the weight of which is supported by the water in which it swims, and taking the naked strain of a deadweight lure which has to be hurled through the air with appreciable force. Shops are full of spinning-rods of all sorts and sizes—including the new glass rods, some of which are ghastly and some of which have a wonderfully good, slow, swinging action that makes them ideal for lobbing out heavy pike lures. If you care to buy yourself a ferrule of the appropriate size and a bit of greenheart about a foot long, you can make yourself a spinning tip to fit on your float-fishing rod and convert it, at a pinch, into a spinning-rod. It is not very difficult for someone who is good with his hands, and methodical, to turn a short spinning-rod of greenheart. You can buy complete kits of parts which you can easily assemble yourself into a rod the equal, or almost the equal, of a shop-sold job—if you will take it very slowly and carefully.

If you are buying or making a spinning-rod, I should recommend a short one—about six feet long. You may be converted to a longer rod later—a long rod has some advantages when it comes to controlling a fish—but I must say I personally find a short six-footer, or even a five-footer, very handy and very efficient. Certainly a single-handed rod for me, if I had to choose between the two—even though after years of intermittent fixed-spool spinning I am back on the old centre-pin and the multiplier. Such a rod can cost you anything from a few shillings to quite a lot of pounds. It is not a terribly important instrument, the spinning-rod; it need not be of such high quality as a fly-rod, which carries vastly worse stresses all the time. I should start with a pretty rough old rod, if I were you, until I had learned to cast accurately and fairly far.

19. Fish That Take a Spinning Lure

ALL PREDATORY fish will on occasion take a spinning lure. That is to say, for our purposes, pike, perch, trout, chub. (The few others need not concern us since it is highly unlikely that we shall meet them.)

All the lures that are thrown out by a spinning-rod and reel are called spinning lures, roughly: but in fact they fall into three classifications. Lures that truly spin, revolving in the water owing to the action of the spinning vanes that work exactly like a propeller in reverse. Lures that rotate irregularly, flopping around in the water—such as spoons. Finally, plugs, that do not revolve at all.

One of the most popular, and the most deadly, of spinning lures, is the dead bait. Smallish fish, from minnows to four-ounce roach, either freshly caught and killed or preserved in a solution of formalin, are mounted on a spinning flight (see Figure 7). This consists, usually, of a pin which is pushed down the dead fish's throat, with two celluloid spinning vanes set at an angle on either side. The fish is whipped firmly to the spinning flight by thread or wire. One company sells natural baits which have been coated with a soft, pliable, but practically indestructible plastic substance (called the Pliquatic bait). For pike, you might choose the dace, the bleak, the roach, the gudgeon. For perch, the minnow or the bleak. For trout and chub, the minnow.

For perch and chub, spin straight and fast in mid water. For pike, spin as slowly as you dare, low down in the water. Search the likely lies as you have been told.

Artificial spinning lures take as many forms as there are
natural creatures that swim—multiplied by some dozens. There
are so-called 'Devon minnows,' which are really streamlined
tubes of metal that sink well and swim die-straight. There are

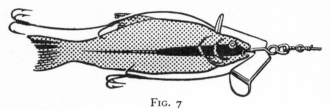

FIG. 7

spoons galore—spoons being, as the name might suggest,
spoon-shaped pieces of beaten metal which flop around rather
irregularly in the water. I have lots of faith in the old spoon as a
bait for pike; either the simple old-fashioned spoon which is
just a spoon, or the variations on a spoon such as the Horton-
Evans 'Vibro,' a very deadly weapon, and the Hardy spoon.
The 'Colorado,' the Holroyd-Smith, and very many others are
deadly at times. You can see as many as you like in any tackle
shop. And you can make your own. (There is a really brilliant
device called the 'Minnomold' by means of which you can make
an endless supply of 'Devon minnows.')

Remember that a revolving lure tends to twist the line.
Never use one without incorporating in your tackle, somewhere
between reel-line and lure, two swivels, and an anti-kink lead
that swims like a keel and *makes* one of the swivels work. This
is called the spinning trace. (See Figure 8.)

Remember, too, that the same basic rules guide the spinner
and the float fisher. *Present your lure to the fish where the fish
expects to find his food.* Remember that only two fish wantonly
and deliberately disport themselves in the full force of the
current—the sprightly dace and the dour barbel (neither of

which is caught by spinning, of course.) All other fish like to get out of the main current—but not too far out. Spin fast, spin slow, spin high, spin low. Search your water thoroughly before giving it up as a bad job. Spinning is not just a matter of tossing

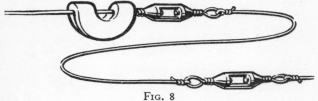

FIG. 8

out a lure and winding it back in—it is a matter of searching the water with great cunning and concentration. It is a lovely form of fishing, lovely to watch and exciting to practise. It keeps you warm on a cold day, interested always even on a dull day. It pays big dividends.

I have only been able to give you the roughest outline of an idea of what spinning is: there are innumerable refinements that make it fascinating to me, and to very many more. But I cannot leave the subject without a reference to plug-fishing. This is roughly classed as spinning, and indeed you use just the same tackle and go through the same motions. But in fact a plug does not revolve in the water. The plug—an American invention I believe—is a piece of wood (sometimes plastic) shaped very roughly like a fish, with a diving vane fixed to its head and one or perhaps two large hooks (double or treble) hanging from it. As it is reeled in, the pressure of water on the diving vane sends it deeper; as the pressure is reduced, it wobbles uncertainly to the surface. The large tail hook acts as a sort of wild, contrary rudder. The whole result is an action in the water that is exactly like the action of an injured, sickly little fish. You always reel a plug in with an uneven motion—a quick turn, a momentary stop, a slow turn, a quick turn, and so on. So the depth and the plane of movement of the plug is changing the whole time, crazily. There is nothing that looks quite so lifelike in the water as a well-designed plug. Pike when they are feeding cannot resist them.

I should like you to read Mr Thurlow Craig's books on spinning. I know none better.

PART VI: FLY-FISHING

<<<<<<<<<<<<<<<<<<<<<<<<<<<<<<<<<<<<<<

20. General Information

<<<<<<<<<<<<<<<<<<<<<<<<<<<<<<<<<<<<<<

IN A LITTLE BOOK that is meant only to introduce a beginner to the fun and fascination of fishing, I can only spare one brief chapter for the whole magic realm of fly-fishing—as I could only spare a few pages for the roughest of rough outlines of spinning. There are very many fine books on both of these subjects, and I am sure that when you begin to settle down in fishing and decide what branch of it really attracts you most, you will find out those books for yourselves. However, I can say this: there is no deep mystery about fly-fishing. Anyone who can catch fish with float tackle can catch fish on the fly. You will meet people who talk of fly-fishing with bated breath, or very nearly, as if it were some holy of holies that only brilliant specialists learned in the magic art can enter. That is rubbish. True, you can go on learning about fly-fishing all your life, and no one ever knows all there is to be known about it. But you can start catching fish on the fly within half an hour of tying your very first fly to a cast. No—better than that. Within five minutes. One of my pupils, a man of seventy who had never touched a fishing rod of any kind before, did just that.

And oh! what delight there is in store for you! I could almost wish that I were beginning all over again in the loveliest, the most delicate, and (in my humble opinion) the most satisfying of all branches of the art of angling. Truly I love all branches of the sport, but for me there is no pleasure quite equal to the joy of casting an artificial fly—itself a creation of beauty and loving care—on the pearl-bright surface of the stream. I think that if ever you try fly-fishing and persevere long enough to gain some small proficiency and success in the art, you will return to it with pleasure again and again—even though, like me, you continue to fish as circumstances dictate, using the spinner, the float, even the ledger, as a wise angler should.

What *is* fly-fishing? Well, just as some fish (but not all) will on occasion eat other fish (which the spinner imitates with his spoons and plugs), so some fish (but not all) will on occasion eat waterborne flies, which the fly-fisher imitates. That is the basis of it all. It is a very ancient sport.

To understand fly-fishing you must know something elementary about flies. Don't think of buzzy house-flies and blue-bottles (though even they have their place in the fisher's scheme of things) but of the flies that are 'born' at the bottom of the river. There are many such flies, and some of them are beautiful. They hatch out from eggs laid in the water and pass a great proportion of their lives under water, as little grubs (think of the caterpillar that becomes a butterfly and you will begin to get the idea). When summer comes, the 'nymph,' as it is called, crawls out of the grub and swims to the surface of the water. Arriving at the surface, the shuck or case splits and out crawls the fly. It rides on the surface for a little time, unfolding in the sun (unless it is eaten by a fish), and then it flies ashore. Drying out still further, it sheds its coat again and emerges in its full glory of gossamer wings. Its life is brief, often lasting only one day. The female settles on the water again to lay its eggs, and dies. So the cycle starts all over again. (The male fly usually dies on land.)

These are the flies with which fish are mainly concerned— though there are flies hatched on land which get blown on to the water, and these are equally welcome to surface-feeding fish. Fish are eating flies at all stages of their development—as grubs clinging to the bottoms of reeds and trailing weeds, as nymphs swimming slowly to the surface to hatch out, as 'duns' floating on the surface, resting, before taking flight, as 'spinners' laying their eggs on the surface, and finally as dead or 'spent' flies drifting downstream awash in the surface film.

Since at various times the angler tries to imitate all these stages of fly life, it follows that sometimes he fishes his artificial fly sunk beneath the surface to represent the nymph, and sometimes he fishes it floating on the surface to represent the mature dun or the dying or dead spinner. The first kind of fishing is called 'wet-fly' fishing; the second kind, 'dry-fly' fishing.

There is another category of artificial flies, which has no counterpart in nature (though this does not prevent such flies from catching many fish). This is the category of the 'fancy' wet or sunk flies which imitate no fly that ever flew, but, rather, a tiny fish. These 'flies' are generally flashy, bright flies tied of vivid feathers and with something of silver or gold tinsel or wire in them. There is nothing whatever wrong with using such lures, of course, any more than there is anything unsporting in using a spinning lure. But it is only called 'fly-fishing' by courtesy. (All salmon flies come into this category—they are all taken for living creatures, presumably shrimps or tiny fish. Salmon do not seem to eat flies proper; or at any rate, not very often.) The first thing you need to learn now is how to cast a fly. You see, it is a problem entirely different from the problem of casting a float and weighted cast, or a spinning lure. In both of those cases there is a real, appreciable weight available to draw the line out: it is actual weight which you are casting or throwing, and the lighter the line the better, within the limits of reasonable safety. But in the case of fly-fishing there is virtually no weight in the fly whatever. So how can you throw something that has no weight? Try throwing a feather: it will not get far, however strong you are.

This problem is solved by the use of the heavy line. A fly line has vastly more weight and bulk than is needed to hold a fish.

You throw *the line*, and the line carries the fly. Think of a cowboy flicking out a stock whip (which tapers down to a fine, light tail) and you will see how it works.

To throw a fly, then, you need a heavy line—a line with enough weight to carry well through the air. That is the first requirement and it cannot be dodged. The second requirement, just as vital, is a rod flexible enough to be 'worked' by the weight of the line. A really stiff rod will not throw a fly well. (By the same token, a really *horribly* whippy rod will not throw a fly far.) You need, in fact, a fly rod, and there is no getting round that. Fly rods are made in every imaginable size and weight and almost every known material, including steel and glass. You must aim to get a rod and line which balance one another. I can only say that, and hope that the salesman in the shop where you buy your first fly-fishing outfit loves the sport and will see that you are fixed up with a properly matched set. (The reel really doesn't matter : almost any old reel will do.) Much the best thing for you to do is to buy a second-hand greenheart fly rod, as short as you like. A big rod is not 'happy'—it is not working properly —until you have out enough line to bring out its latent power, whereas a little light rod is working perfectly happily with half a dozen yards or so of line in use. And you want to start your fly-fishing with short casts—you can adventure long casting when you feel you are on top of the job. (I myself use a seven-foot rod most of the time.)

To make a cast, go out on to the lawn or common, or any patch of grass, with your rod set up and the line drawn through the rings. Tie a tiny fragment of rag to the end of the line so that you will see where it falls. Pull out about eight yards and lay that line on the grass in front of you.

To cast, raise the rod smoothly but sharply until it is vertical. If you do this with sufficient pep, the line will rise and fly out in the air behind you. When it straightens out you will feel a slight tug at the rod tip. But it's better at first to turn your head and watch the line stream out behind you. When the line is about to be fully extended—just a fraction before it is stretched tight—bring the rod forward and downwards, smoothly but strongly. The line will curl and go out forward again. Try to remember that cowboy cracking his whip.

Two vital points. Never let the rod go back farther than the vertical. It comes up vertical and stays there. Of course, the tip will be bent slightly backwards by the pull of the line, but only the tip. The butt must remain vertical in your hand. (Figure 9 shows the grip for a fly rod.) Remember to make a pause at the top—a pause to let the back cast straighten out before you begin to impel the line forward again. If you wait too long, the line will fall to the ground behind you. If you don't wait long enough, you will hear a loud crack and that will be the last of your fly, snapped off as neatly as with a knife. Rhythm is everything. You practise and practise; and sometimes you get fairly expert, sometimes you stay a plodder.

That is basic casting. Once you can perform that overhead cast with fair proficiency, getting the line out nice and straight for a fair distance—ten yards is plenty—and aiming it right too, then you can go fly-fishing. There are several other fancy casts, all very useful at times, but this is only to introduce you to the fundamentals.

I dare say you will manage the rod and reel, but that fly line may be a problem. Fly lines are desperately expensive. They are made of silk or nylon and, curiously enough, although nylon is fine for every other sort of line it does not make very good fly lines. At least, that is the opinion of many experienced anglers, including me. It is too light and too supple.

Lines are also made tapered or level. Tapered lines are very nice—obviously they help you to drop a fly lightly on the water without alarming the fish—but they are about two to three times as dear as level lines, and you can manage very well with a level line.

FIG. 9

If, as I suggested early in this book, you start off with a good old second-hand greenheart fly rod, you will find that you can use it for float fishing and ledgering, for spinning at a pinch—though only light spinning, certainly not pike spinning—and now for the final joy, fly-fishing itself. That certainly is an economy.

To the end of the heavy fly line you attach a cast, of course. This again can be an expensive affair of gut, tapered down to a fine point. Very pleasant it makes casting. But you can manage perfectly well with two or three yards of plain nylon, 3X or 4X. Loop it and tie it to the line with the knots shown in Chapter 23.

Tie your fly to the end of the cast with the turle knot shown in Chapter 23, and you are ready for fly-fishing.

Dry fly or wet fly? It's an old problem—almost an old battle. It hardly matters, honestly. Some just happen to prefer one way, some prefer another. If there are flies hatching out on the surface of the water, and fish are rising to suck them in, making those rings and dimples and sipping noises which to me are the most thrilling sights and sounds of the waterside—why, then, *of course* fish the dry fly. Smear the wings or hackles of your fly with a trace of that Mucilin with which you grease your line to make it float, and keep the fly buoyant by repeatedly 'false casting' between shots—that only means waving it to and fro in the air without letting it touch the water.

If you are casting to rising fish, using, of course, the dry fly, you must cast upstream. Crawl along until you are within your own casting range of the fish and aim to drop the fly a few feet above him—or a few feet above where you saw the ring. If your shot is about right, the fly will float down right past his nose, he will rise and suck it in, you will tighten up on him, and carry on just as if you were playing any fish on any tackle. You know how, now.

But if there is no visible rise and you decide to fish the sunk fly in search of fish feeding beneath the surface on nymphs, you do not grease your fly. On the contrary, tying on a sparsely hackled wet fly, you wet it thoroughly to make sure it will sink. You can cast this upstream, if you like, aiming it at spots of quiet water where you think a fish may be lying—in the small patches of calm water above and below boulders, in eddies and backwaters, and so on. Since the fly sinks, you will not see it taken. You soon develop a new 'instinct' to help you—or perhaps you don't in which case you never come to enjoy upstream wet-fly fishing very much! It is without doubt the most difficult of all fishing arts to acquire. You sometimes see the cast checked faintly as it floats downstream, you may see a flash as a fish darts at your fly—that is as much indication as you will get. No, it is a hard though (for some) a very profitable business. Perhaps you had better stick to dry-fly—or wet-fly fish 'across and down.'

This is the very old-fashioned way of fishing a fly. Many sneer at it now, but it is still useful. You cast your wet fly almost directly across the stream, or slightly downstream. Holding the line between the forefinger and thumb of your left hand, you let the submerged fly swing round in the current until the line is pointing directly downstream. Now, if you have felt nothing, draw it back towards you with sharpish, definite tugs, drawing in about three inches of line with each tug, and spacing the tugs about three seconds apart or a bit less. If you are lucky, you will feel a pull at the line. Strike instantly.

That is the bare outline of fly-fishing.

21. Flies and Fish

THE CLASSIC fish that are taken on flies or so-called flies are, of course, trout, sea-trout, salmon, and grayling. But in addition to those lordly fish (about which I am not writing, since it is not over-likely that you will spend your apprenticeship fishing for them) there are a number of sporting coarse fish that will often, in summer, rise to the fly. These are the chub, the dace, the rudd, the roach—and sometimes the perch.

There is a special kind of fly-fishing often practised for chub, which does not call for a fly line or a fly rod. You use your ordinary float tackle—without the float. This is called dibbing or dapping. It is hardly fly-fishing as I know it, but the lure is undoubtedly a fly.

If by careful reconnaissance you locate a shoal of chub sauntering up and down under an overhanging bush or tree, on the prowl for insects dropping from the branches, retire forthwith and approach again with great stealth, armed for battle. Remove your float, tie a big buzzy sort of chub fly—a Zulu or a Soldier Palmer or a Red Palmer—to the end of your cast. Pinch on one shot an inch or two above the fly. Reel in line until you have a few yards hanging from the rod top, and wind that carefully round the tip. Then insinuate your rod tip through the branches of the bush until it is directly over the chub. Unwind the line by turning the rod. The weight of the shot will carry the fly down. Don't just rest it on the surface—let it plop down the last inch or two with quite a little splash, just as if it were a real beetle or caterpillar that had mised his footing on a branch and fallen into the water. I hope a chub will grab it for you—they often do. How you play him and withdraw the rod through the bush is your worry. No one can help you in print.

Chub will take the dry or wet fly fished in the orthodox manner, too, very satisfactorily in high summer when most fish are sulking. Dry flies: Zulu, the Palmers, Sedge, Coachman, Coch-y-Bonddhu. Wet flies: Same, plus Butcher, Alexandra, Invicta.

Dace may be had on a tiny Black Gnat or Wickham's Fancy, preferably dry, but sometimes wet. Any small fly will do for any of the coarse fish, rudd, roach, dace. I should say that a Black Gnat or Wickham's Fancy is as good as anything.

Perch are sometimes to be had on a sunk, gaudy fly, which they almost certainly take for a tiny fish. Such flies as the Butcher, Alexandra, Invicta, Mallard and Claret, Teal and Red, Teal and Green—or a small gaudy salmon fly or sea-trout lure —fished through the water in a series of jerks, will sometimes bring about their downfall. (Even pike are occasionally caught on such a fly.)

When fishing still water with the wet fly, of course, you keep it moving in small jerks all the time, until it is fished right back to you.

PART VII:
THE FIXED-SPOOL REEL

∞∞∞∞∞∞∞∞∞∞∞∞∞∞∞∞∞∞∞∞∞∞∞∞∞∞∞∞∞∞∞∞

22. Using a Fixed-spool Reel

∞∞∞∞∞∞∞∞∞∞∞∞∞∞∞∞∞∞∞∞∞∞∞∞∞∞∞∞∞∞∞∞

WHEN I FIRST wrote this little book in 1953, I said very little about the fixed-spool reel, though even then it was fast becoming a pretty popular tool. But I was writing for those who wanted to try their hands at fishing but didn't want to invest a lot of money in tackle until they were quite sure they liked it—and at that time the fixed-spool reel was jolly expensive, even the cheapest models costing several pounds. So I skipped lightly over the subject, and indeed it is perfectly true that you can fish well and happily for a lifetime without even seeing a fixed-spool reel. Izaak Walton never saw *any* kind of reel, though he'd vaguely heard of the newfangled 'winch.' He did all right.

But now, in 1957—when I am having to revise this book because so many thousands of people have been good enough to buy it that the publisher has sold out and we must produce another edition—now, I say, the fixed-spool reel has established itself so ubiquitously, and has become so cheap, that no book even for beginners would be complete without a chapter on it. One great firm has actually produced a reel which simplifies the fixed-spool principle down to the final degree of simplification—and they only charge 15s. 6d.! That apart, there are several reels on the market which embody all the gubbins and gimmicks and gadgets and still retail at prices like 30s. and 50s. Moreover, it seems to me, from all I hear as I wander around from tackle shop to tackle shop, and at the waterside, and in the mail which I get as an angling writer—it seems to me that no lad considers himself fixed up, nowadays, unless he owns a fixed-spool reel. So we must look into it.

Who invented the fixed-spool reel? The devil, say many fine fishermen such as my friend Mr C. V. Hancock of the *Birmingham Post*, whose delightful book, *Rod in Hand*, you really ought to read one day. The devil, eh? Why? Well, there is a sort of splendid old reactionary who does not believe in everything being made easy. According to this brand of thinker, if a thing is worth doing at all it is worth doing dexterously, with craftsmanlike skill. If you want to get a lure to a fish, you ought to have to *work* at it. It *ought* to be difficult, because if it's easy there is no satisfaction in doing it, and taking fish becomes only a degree less dreary than buying them off a slab.

That, very roughly, sums up the emotional resistance of many fine fly-fishermen, old-fashioned spinners, and others to the fixed-spool reel. Because—in a word—the fixed-spool reel makes casting so easy that even a school-teacher or television critic or editor can do it, after five minutes' tuition.

Mark you, I can understand perfectly the attitude of those who claim that the devil invented the fixed-spool reel. I don't quite share their scorn, but I know what lies behind it. The fact is that before the invention of the fixed-spool reel it was devilishly difficult to cast a very light lure. It was almost impossible. If you wanted to fish for trout in 'thin' water—the shallow, clear water of high summer—you had to add chunks of lead to your trace before you could get the old kind of centre-pin reel revolving. It didn't go out very far and it hit the water with an awful splash and plonk and as often as not it fouled the bottom, and anyway the trout were hiding under stones long before it reached the spot where they *had* been lying.

So to catch trout in such conditions, which are common in summer, you more or less *had* to learn to fish the fly. You had to be good at it, too. This was excellent for the stock of trout but not too good for the angler's self-esteem if he didn't happen to like fly-fishing, as some poor chaps don't. But along came the fixed-spool reel and immediately any ham-fisted mutt could throw a feather-weight minnow, *or a worm*, twenty or thirty or

FIG. 10

even forty yards, with a mere flick of the wrist. It was *too* tempting. Legions of 'threadliners,' as they were called, descended on the trout waters of Britain and pretty near emptied them of fish. (I know for sure of one man who caught fifty-two trout in fifty-two casts.) It got so bad that very soon most associations and clubs and private fishery owners banned the fixed-spool reel—in fact, banned spinning—for trout. Quite right, too.

Salmon fishing was also affected, very much for the worse.

For the introduction of the fixed-spool reel made it easy for chaps who couldn't be bothered to learn how to use a centre-pin reel—or a fly rod. With a fixed-spool reel and midget rod these chaps began spinning for salmon and they were deadly success- ful—so far as *hooking* fish went. But since the early fixed-spool reels only allowed of very fine lines being used, and since, too, the early threadliners hadn't a lot of practice in playing big fish on fine tackle, a great many breakages occurred. A great many noble great fish were swimming around miserably with a treble hook stuck in their jaws and trailing many yards of absurdly fine line. I can well understand that good, sound sportsmen damned the invention of the fixed-spool reel heartily.

But now, having put the old case against the fixed-spool reel as fairly as I can, I must tell you something about its undoubted virtues and many advantages. For they *are* many. It is a per- fectly brilliant invention and it is here to stay. The fixed-spool reel has a place in every angler's tackle cupboard. As I said, you can fish through a lifetime happily without one, but to disregard the invention as if it had never happened is more or less on a par with disregarding the aeroplane and the motor-car. Very well, lots of people would like to. But there it is.

The principle on which the fixed-spool works is easy to understand, and it is easy to learn to use it—after a fashion. Real skill and command come only with practice and knowledge of what is really involved. Let's begin at the beginning

Any ordinary reel is a true winch. The axis of the spool lies at right angles to the rod. You turn the handles and line is wound on to the spool just like winding a bucket up a well. And, in reverse, when you make a cast the weight of the lure, plus any lead on the trace, has to start the spool revolving just like the bucket going down. And to overcome the inertia of the spool some appreciable force and/or weight is needed. But if you use too much force and/or weight, and fail to control the revolving spool, it tends to revolve faster than line is being drawn off. The line bags and stands up from the spool and is then trapped and tucked in under loose coils, and the result is an almighty tangle known far and wide as a 'bird's nest.'

Now with the fixed-spool reel no such thing can happen. The fixed-spool is fixed: it never revolves. Moreover, its axis lies in the same plane as the axis of the rod—that is to say, the lip of the spool is at right-angles to the rod. When you make a cast, the line is pulled off over the lip of the spool in coils. There is no resistance except the trifling friction of the line itself on the lip of the spool. When you have made your cast, you begin to turn the handle and a thing called a 'flier,' which you pushed out of the way to make your cast, comes into action again and catches hold of the line. As you turn the handle, the flier lays the line neatly back on to the spool.

A further refinement. In order that the line may be laid back neatly on the spool and not all bunched up in one part, the spool itself is geared to give a slight up-and-down movement, so that the line is laid on it properly all the way from front to back.

There is one further refinement, the slipping clutch. This has probably caused more misunderstanding than anything in angling. Somewhere in the winding mechanism—it varies from reel to reel—a friction clutch is incorporated. You can adjust it by turning a knob or disk, varying the grip of the clutch from solid drive (locked) to a very light, slipping drive. The idea behind this is that if the fish makes a sudden heavy plunge you cannot be taken unawares and broken. Instead, the spool slips round and line is drawn off.

Theoretically, then, in open water no fish can break you, however fine the line, provided the clutch is so set that the reel will slip and 'give line' at a pressure slightly below what is needed to break the line. This device has led to innumerable misunderstandings and to some pretty dubious angling. On the one hand, enormous fish *have*, indubitably, been landed on very fine lines. But on the other hand, many anglers have been tempted to go for big fish with absurdly fine lines. There is no need for this and no point in it. The early fixed-spool reels would only accommodate very fine lines, but nowadays you can get a reel which will take almost any weight of line you choose, and it is good sense to match the line strength to the quarry—and the strength of the current.

Now to business. You can use the fixed-spool reel for virtually anything except fly-fishing. You can use it for float-fishing, for ledgering, for trotting the stream, and—I almost said preeminently—for spinning. You can use it for sea fishing, too, but that is beyond the scope of this book.

Notes on use of the fixed-spool reel fall into three parts—how to cast, how to hook a fish, and how to play a fish.

It might appear that nobody could possibly need advice on how to make a cast with a fixed-spool reel, it is so easy. All you have to do is pick up the line on the inside of the tip of the forefinger, push the pick-up wire out of operation, and make your cast. But, in fact, I have seen a lot of anglers cutting down the distance they ought to be able to cast through one very common and simple mistake. Many people pick up the line in the crook at the first joint of the finger. It seems a natural thing to do, but in fact a fine line tends to stick in the crook and you lose quite a bit of distance through that. Merely pick up the line on the pad of the finger—then it will fly off in a spritely way as soon as you make your cast.

As for hooking a fish, now, remember that you have that slipping clutch. If you have set it properly and if your hook is sharp, fine in the wire, and with a modest little barb, you will find no difficulty in making it penetrate. But if the above things aren't *exactly* as they should be, you will quite possibly find that the hook does not penetrate above the barb, and that fish may well jump off. My own trick is to trap the spool solid with one finger when I strike. Just for a vital moment, convert it from a slipping-clutch reel to a locked reel—just for that moment while you strike. Then the hook will go in over the barb and you can release your finger-pressure on the spool.

As for playing a fish on a fixed-spool reel, there are two schools of thought. One school says: Adjust the clutch pressure so that the fish can just about take off line below the critical breaking point, and play it at that. The second school of thought, to which I belong myself, says: Throw off almost ALL clutch pressure, and control the reel *solely* by finger-pressure on the rim of the spool.

It sounds absurd, if not impossible. But, in fact, it is a very sound way of controlling a fish. The fingers we were born with are—or should be—much more sensitive than any bit of engineering. If you control the fish's runs by finger-pressure on the spool *and* win back line by the method known as 'pumping,' you will have complete mastery of your fish and no fear of breakage. For by this means you can vary the pressure on the fish, as needed, from nothing to the greatest the line is capable of standing—all in an instant, without need to fiddle with mechanical gadgets.

My own practice is to fish with the clutch set so light that it is only *just* working, that is to say, just bringing the lure along (I'm thinking of spinning now, but the same general principle applies to every form of fishing). When I feel my fish take, I trap the spool solid with a finger and strike hard enough to get the hook home above the barb. Now the fish's immediate reaction is flight—off he tears. But in a split second I release all pressure from him—simply by taking my finger off the spool.

What does the fish do? Ten to one, he stops running. He feels no pressure and therefore he has nothing to fight against— nothing to run away *from*. He is bewildered from the start. He literally doesn't know which way to turn.

As soon as the fish has steadied down you start to shorten line—to reel him in, that is. This you can only safely do by pumping. In fact, pumping is a method that should always be used with every type of reel. It is kindest to rod and reel.

Imagine that your rod is pointing up in the air, at an angle of about sixty degrees. You start to reel in, and all that happens is that your rod tip is pulled down to the water. Exactly. *Then* you trap the spool with your finger and heave the rod up again. That way you gain a yard or two. Repeat the process as often as is necessary—ever wary and ready, should you feel the heavy plunge of a fish, to release your finger-pressure on the spool and let him run a bit, if he wants to.

I don't want to make a thing of this finger-control method, particularly, because I do know lots of chaps who get along quite well with a moderate clutch pressure and 'normal' playing methods—that is to say, they wind in as long as they can get away with it, and if the fish makes a strong run they either keep on winding or, at most, hang on to the reel handle, while the fish drags off line against the clutch pressure. It works, no doubt about it: but it is very much less effective than throwing the clutch pressure almost right off and controlling the fish entirely by finger-pressure on the spool.

Remember that a fixed-spool reel is also, as a general thing, a multiplier. That is to say, it is geared up, so that every revolution of the handle gives you about three or more turns of the flier round the spool. So you get a pretty fast rate of recovery. This is *for* you when spinning a light bait upstream in shallow water—such a deadly way of catching trout and sea trout and salmon in high summer. But it is *against* you when it comes to playing a fish, remember that.

Undoubtedly the fixed-spool reel makes it possible to fish spots which are inaccessible even to the most highly skilled angler using a centre-pin reel. With it, you can flick a light lure underneath overhanging boughs, into tight corners—and over prodigious distances.

The float-fisher finds that he can toss out a toothpick float, single shot, and maggot a real fishing distance. The light ledger expert can reach the 'middle of the pool.' When I am ledgering, or fishing a bait with no lead on the bottom, as for carp, I leave the pick-up wire open and watch the line—when it is being drawn steadily off the spool, seize the rod, snap the pick-up arm into action by a swift turn of the handle, lock the reel momentarily when you feel the fish, and make your decisive strike.

The reel is not so well adapted to long corking or trotting down the stream, but it *can* be used with success. The technique is to make your cast out into the current and leave the pick-up arm in the 'Off' position. Trap the line at the spool's rim by a finger of the right hand, and let go a coil, or a coil or two, often enough to keep your float trotting nicely downstream. The snag is that when the float goes under you have to whip the handle round pretty fast in order to make your strike before the fish has let go the lure. Still, though I much prefer the centre-pin reel for trotting, the fixed-spool reel *will* work.

Fixed-spool reels come in several sizes these days, but however big they are, one thing stays true of them all. When the level of line falls appreciably below the rim of the spool, casting distance falls off. So keep the spool nicely full—use an elastic band to hold the line snug when not in use.

I should mention that the fixed-spool reel has yet another characteristic which does not apply to revolving-spool reels. The finer the gauge of line on the spool, the more easily it comes off and the farther you can cast with a given weight. However, there is no need to use ridiculously fine lines any more. The development of monofilament nylon has made it possible to get a line of quite fair strength—say, 5-lb. breaking strain—which is jolly near invisible in the water. So the need to chance your arm with gossamer threads of 2-lb. breaking strain is a thing of the past. (Unless you are fishing for wary roach.)

Never forget that a line has one strength dry and another strength when soaked—usually far less than the dry strength.

On a spool of I.C.I. 'Luron' on my desk I notice that it quotes 6 lb. as the dry breaking strain, but only 4 lb. as the wet breaking strain. Bear this in mind. And, moreover, a knotted line is just as strong as the knot—and the best knot in the world only gives you about 85 per cent at best of the line's full breaking strain.

There has grown up the cult of the 'threadline rod' to match the fixed-spool reel. Usually it is a terrible little thing seven feet long, with a stiff butt and a whippy top. No doubt about it, to flick out a lure (when spinning) you need a quick-acting top joint: but this trend has gone much too far, in my opinion. Look for a rod that has a bit of action right down to the butt. It might not cast quite so fast and far as a tip-actioned rod, but it will play a fish more safely, and last a lot longer, too.

When casting with a fixed-spool reel—especially when spinning—the bit of line nearest to the lure takes a terrible beating. All, or almost all, the strain of the cast is taken by the bit of line where it joins the lure, or weight. Watch this carefully. Break off a few yards every day—or every time you land a big fish. Thus you will find the line gradually dwindling on the spool until its level is well below the lip. There's nothing for it then but to strip off all the line and knot or whip on a bit of backing—enough to bring the level up again. Too bad, but there it is. Press on, laddie. This is progress.

Seriously, I wouldn't be without my fixed-spool reel (I own the popular model shown in the illustration). It very greatly enlarges your scope for action. For heavy spinning, for fishing for salmon and big pike, I still stick to the old centre-pin reel or the multiplier. But for lighter lures the fixed-spool reel cuts out the real hard labour and the hit-and-miss, and makes me feel a maestro. It makes anybody feel a maestro. Like independent front suspension for cars, it has its bitter reactionary critics —but it is here to stay, and rightly, on the strength of its undeniable brilliance.

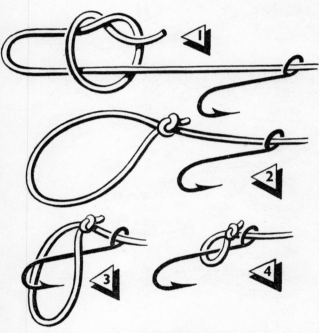

FIG. 11. The 'Turle' Knot

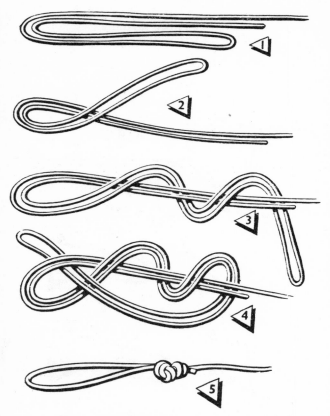

FIG. 12. Looping nylon—the 'Blood Bight'

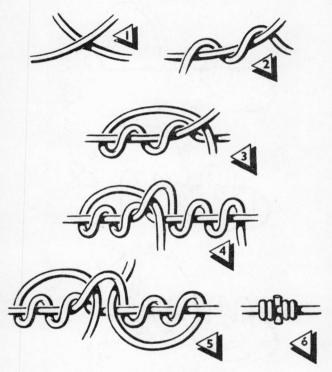

FIG. 13. The 'Double Blood' Knot

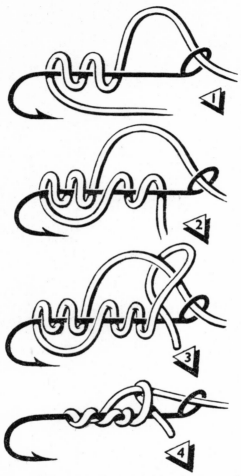

FIG. 14. Heavy-duty Knot-to-hook—the 'Lenwade'

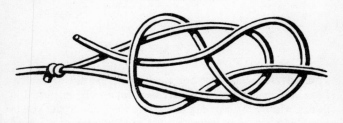

FIG. 15. The 'Figure of Eight' Knot—for attaching the end of the reel line to the looped cast

POSTSCRIPT

I DID NOT write this little book to whet your appetite for fishing. I assumed that you were already beginning to be interested in fishing when you bought it, and I have tried only to put you in touch with the basic requirements and techniques of the usual ways of angling in this country. There is no *need* for me, or anyone else, to try to kindle enthusiasm in you. It will kindle itself, a steady and enduring flame of enthusiasm, as your experience grows. Of that I am sure.

Very probably, when you have fished for a few years, you will come to love one practice of angling better than all others; one time of year, and even one sort of fish. Very well. Much happiness may it bring you. All I ask is that you give as many aspects of angling a trial as you possibly can, before you 'settle down' in your chosen branch.

I am a 'general angler' myself; a proud title, my friends, even though salmon fishers might smile to hear me boast of it. I fish here and there and anywhere, with anything, for anything: and it is all solace, delight, and adventure. But I confess that I have my favourites, too, as we are all entitled to. I am torn between two loves: I cannot decide which is dearest—and, thank heaven, there is no need to decide. In two sorts and two seasons I find my own abounding happiness.

Not for me the drowsy haze of high summer, not even the luminous charm of autumn; lovely though both be. For me, the happiness of the first fly-fishing in April, when trout rise boldly after their long immunity, and the world is waking. And the other great joy . . . so different, a different world, iron-bare and bold and beautiful with all the foliage stripped away . . . the loveliness and the pounding exhilaration of the red-eyed winter's day, when I stride and march the margins of the great meres and the steel-dark river, hunting the desperate pike as the pike hunts his prey. Yes, I should be torn indeed to decide between the two. Heaven be praised again, for life and strength and health and hope, for trout and pike, for spring and winter, for fishing all my days.

M. W.

EAST CLANDON, 1953.